COOK
CLEVER

SHIVI RAMOUTAR

COOK CLEVER

ONE CHOP \ **NO WASTE** \ **ALL TASTE**

HarperCollins*Publishers*

For my Cake, Icing and Cherry:
Milesy, Ots and Hazel

CONTENTS

COOK

To prepare a meal, by mixing, combining and/or heating ingredients.

CLEVER

Showing inventiveness or originality; ingenious.

Anyone who knows me knows that I love dedicating a whole day to lovingly recreating authentic recipes. I can spend hours poring over feasts and menus from one of those absolutely stunning books, one that is filled to the brim with rich history, touching family anecdotes and new (well, new to me) ingredients and methods that are well worth the time often spent on them. So, this book is not one of those.

This book is all about the day-to-day. It's about delicious simplicity, but the point is that simplicity does not have to mean boring. My hope is that this book will bring you out of the food rut that you can often find yourself in when you're stuck in a routine of cooking the same meals day-in day-out. Think *exciting*, but also easy. So how will this book make you cook clever?

My aim with this book is to remove the difficulty and effort often associated with cooking by using simple, but nonetheless 'ingenious' shortcuts, ingredients and techniques. Isn't that something we are all after, in every aspect of life? While I may not be able to make your job, your love life or learning to the play the piano easier, what I can offer you with *Cook Clever* is this: recipes, tips and tricks that effortlessly pave the way to creating easy, exciting home-cooked meals. This is the way I *truly* cook when I am at home.

Let's look at what we're trying to avoid:

- Slaving over a chopping board, finely dicing piles of veg while the kids (or significant other) are stocking up on snacks behind me because whatever I'm cooking is taking too long to prepare.

- Finding leftover ingredients that have been forgotten at the back of the fridge that ultimately end up in the bin. The main culprits are lone courgettes, handfuls of mushrooms, half bags of spinach and herbs, and half tins of sweetcorn or beans.

- Having to weigh everything out to the gram, then screaming to the high heavens when my scales run out of battery in the middle of a recipe. (Tell me that this happens to you too?!).

- Complex cooking methods to frown over and demystify and a host of UFOs (unidentifiable food objects) – ingredients that you've never heard of or can't find at your local supermarket.

- Endless prep that uses every bowl, pan and utensil in your kitchen, ultimately leading to towering piles of washing-up.

Alright, enough of the dreary scenarios; let me tell you how I set about answering these common complaints. I've done all the thinking, testing, tasting and honing for you and created a collection of *Cook Clever* recipes with this format:

MINIMUM INPUT
(ingredients, prep
time, mess and waste)

+

(delicious, colourful,
wholesome,
world-flavoured)
MAXIMUM OUTPUT

This is how I truly cook at home in those mundane or mad moments of life. This book encompasses a lot of the ideas I set out in *The Ice Kitchen*: maximising on convenience, cutting down on waste and saving money and time. I've noted which recipes are freezer-friendly, so that you can use *The Ice Kitchen* method of making double – one for now and (freezing) one for later.

The ingredients in my kitchen are carefully and cleverly chosen to ensure that chopping is kept to an absolute minimum: think spring onions snipped with scissors, mini shallots you can fling in whole rather than dicing onions for days, using whole baby button mushrooms or grating carrots rather than finely chopping them. I love wielding a good kitchen knife and my job means I have to most days. But what I am getting at here is that in the rush and whirlwind of life, when I get home and want an effortlessly delicious meal, snipping, tearing or grating straight into the pan is far less time- and mind-consuming than getting out a chopping board and knife. It also means you can more easily multitask or chat with a loved one while you're prepping.

You'll find me using pastes and spice mixes and other clever time-saving ingredients, like ginger purée, ready-grated cheese and the like, all of which

THERE IS NO WRONG OR RIGHT ANSWER – IT'S WHATEVER WORKS FOR YOU.

can be easily found at your local supermarket. Another bonus is that you'll often be asked to just 'bung it all in' with minimal additional prepping. And you'll rarely need to get the scales out as I've deliberately listed ingredients that come in commonly found packets or sizes – without compromising on quality or flavour. Failing that you'll usually be able to use my 'one mug to rule them all' method of measuring (see page 30).

However, these kinds of clever shortcuts are often where food snobbery can start to sneak in. Which shortcuts are acceptable and which aren't, and where do you draw the line? What may have been fashionable or 'acceptable' does change over time. For example, there was a time when dried mixed herb packets were all the rage, but now they are barely ever called for in recipes. Do you remember the days of powdered mashed potato, the first microwave meals and Sunday Roasts in a tin? Some of you may have cringed at the memory of these; others of you may recall them fondly.

There is no wrong or right answer – it's whatever works for you. For some of you baked beans, jars of ready-made pesto and tins of soup are perfectly acceptable, while others of you will think nothing of putting the time and effort into making your own from scratch. Do you see where I am heading with this? There's no judgement here! Personally I do always make sure that I have some of these in my kitchen, just for those moments where convenience is key. I guess if I have to draw the line on convenience, it is where the shortcut ingredient contains unnecessary additives and chemicals and starts to

THE DISHES I'VE DEVELOPED HAVE REVOLUTIONISED HOW I COOK FOR MY OWN FAMILY, AND HAVE SAVED ME SO MUCH TIME.

taste less and less like the original ingredient. So do I go down the powdered mash route? Probably not. But oven fries? Sign me up!

And what about kitchen basics? Frozen chopped onion? YES! Garlic purée? For me, given how quick and convenient it is to squash a clove in a garlic crusher for that unadulterated pungent aromatic of the real deal, I'd say, nope. However, when it comes to ginger, the effort it takes to peel and grate ginger weighed up against the convenience of the ready-to-go puréed version and the difference in flavour, I'll opt for the supermarket convenience version *most* times. I say most, because if I am recreating a dish from a recipe that calls for a host of particular ingredients, or where ginger takes the starring role, or perhaps where it's used in a more raw state, then grating ginger would certainly be

worth the effort here. I am talking mostly about everyday cooking and the everyday convenience items that would go hand in hand without really compromising flavour.

Yes, I know minimal or no-chop prep sounds like an impossible home cooking challenge but the dishes I've developed have revolutionised how I cook for my own family, and have saved me so much time in an otherwise crazy-busy day. I promise I'm not being reckless here: I have extensively tested out alternative ingredients and found clever substitutions, designing the recipes in such a way that the end result is delightful and doesn't at all sacrifice on flavour, yet is effortless – whatever your level of skill in the kitchen.

You'll notice a lot of *-ish* recipes or versions of complicated classics – think Aubergine Parmigiana or

Chicken Kyiv – that I have simplified while still offering a loving nod to their traditional original. Embrace these wholeheartedly as I promise you they will more than scratch that itch, and I don't need to remind you they'll be as simple as apple pie to make (although probably easier).

For the vegans, vegetarians or flexitarians in your life, you will notice that many of my recipes are meat-free, or give you the option to swap out the meat, reflecting my approach to eating: lots of veg, meat a little less often and when I do eat it the best quality I can afford. Of course, it's not for me to preach to you about your approach to eating, but what I can tell you is that you'll find lots of substitutions and simple swaps to twist the recipes into ones that fit your way of life, and to cater for the preferences and tastes of your loved ones. Whether you want to make more of the recipes veggie, or even add meat to veggie recipes, the substitutions are endless.

Make my meals work for you with whatever you have at hand, using my **fridge forage** tips as inspiration for what to use in a particular recipe.

There is a big nod to waste-free cooking in this collection, with

listed ingredients that take into account typical supermarket-bought amounts, so you won't have to worry about half a tin of chopped tomatoes, or half a carrot here or there. I have also created two useful appendices of **Love Your Leftovers**, which you can easily refer to when you need to use up commonplace leftover ingredients like roast chicken, or sad fridge foraged salad leaves that more often than not end up hitting the bin, as well as a **What to Do With Leftover Ingredients from *Cook Clever* Recipes** where you can see how to elongate the shelf life of the ingredients where the recipe actually does call for a portion or fraction of an ingredient. There are also a few recipes where you can pick and choose ingredients from a list, depending on what you have available, to create quick, nutritious and exciting meals in moments – see Wrapper's Delight (page 118), Fried Rice Mathematics (page 124), Curry in a Hurry (page 138) and Make a Pie of It (page 136), to name a few. These recipes came about during peak lockdown when we were all working from home; my aim was to create simple step-by-step recipes with a clear end result that could be made using any number of ingredients that needed using up or that you just fancied having. I've listed the

IF YOU ARE CLEVER WITH YOUR COOKING, YOU CAN MAKE YOUR INGREDIENTS GO FURTHER AND SAVE MONEY.

possible substitutions, but never feel like you can't go off-piste and wing it with what you have – that's when the magic truly happens and you really *Cook Clever.*

There are some convenience foods, such as jarred peppers or mixed bags of salad and veg, that are more cost-effective to buy (when you factor in the peppers and oil and seasoning to slow roast them, or all the different salad ingredients and the time needed to chop and prepare them), whereas products like pouches of microwave rice or straight-to-wok noodles are often a little more expensive than the less convenient raw ingredient. Remember that you can sometimes save money by buying in bulk or looking for 3 for 2

deals, freezing the unused amount for future meals. But regardless of cost, using ready-to-go options will mean less cooking time (saving on your energy bills), will cut down your time and mean less to wash up. It really is up to you to decide whether the convenient option is more important, at that moment in time (and of course this can change from midweek to weekend, for example) or whether cost is more important. If you would rather cook the noodles from scratch and roast your own peppers, by all means, do so.

Right, I have set out what I'm trying to achieve in creating these recipes, so let's get down to some practical basics. Here are my top tips to Cook Clever.

COOK CLEVER IN / 10

1

PEEL THE ONION

Let's get straight to the nitty-gritty of it. The culprit that often requires the most (sweat and) tears is our dear friend, the onion. Don't get me wrong, there are certain occasions that this layered hero can't be substituted, for example where a recipe calls for caramelisation of onions, or in many Indian dishes where the deep colouring of the onion is key to the flavour profile. But did you know that you can buy ready-chopped onion (fresh or frozen) at the supermarket? If you are happy to throw caution to the wind, another option is to swap your alliums around. I love to substitute spring onions (bulb and all) where a recipe calls for white onion. Instead of dicing, I just use scissors to snip the whole thing straight into the pan – it's less mess and is ready in a snip of the time. If you are happy chopping, but have the 'wrong' onion at home, don't worry about interchanging red for white, or vice versa. (Although, if a recipe calls for raw red onion, note that using raw white will give a harsher flavour, but soaking in iced water can help to remove a little of that acridity.) I also have invested in a mini food chopper, which is just ideal for chopping onions – definitely worthwhile!

2

THE GREATER GRATER

Before you reach for the knife, when called to 'finely dice', think whether you can grate, tear or even use a vegetable peeler to peel the ingredient into slivers instead. Carrots, courgettes, cabbage, garlic and ginger are all perfectly suited to grating. Mushrooms can also be grated, or even torn. For coleslaws and salads I always reach for my vegetable peeler to ensure I get thin strips of salad or veg – it's a perfect method for carrots, cucumber and cabbage, although a mini food chopper can come to the rescue here too!

3 BOUQUET YOUR HERBS

Fresh herbs can really elevate basic dishes to another level of oomph. Taking care with how you store herbs can elongate their life, meaning you always have a meal 'elevator' right at your fingertips – it will also save you money and avoids waste. Fresh soft herbs like coriander, parsley, mint, basil, tarragon and dill should be treated like cut flowers: trim the ends of their stems, remove any brown leaves, pop them in a glass with an inch of water and store in the fridge. For hardier herbs like woody thyme, rosemary and sage, wrap them up like a burrito in a piece of damp kitchen paper then store in the fridge in a resealable freezer bag.

EASY FREEZY

I may have mentioned this somewhere before (check out *The Ice Kitchen!*) but the freezer is a fantastic resource we should make the most of. Any leftover sauces, lemon juice, stock, wine, pesto can be frozen in ice-cube trays and kept for those times that you need to add a little extra (and quick) oomph and flavour to a dish. Sometimes, I siphon off a couple of tablespoons of sauce from a chilli, curry, pasta sauce or stew just so that I can use those as a flavour base in midweek meals needed in a jiffy. And don't forget that those half-tins of chopped tomatoes, chickpeas and tomato pastes can all be frozen. Use ice-cube trays (to freeze tablespoon amounts) or muffin tins for larger portions. Remember that it's more energy efficient to keep your freezer fully stocked, rather than chilling an empty space!

HASTY, PASTE(Y) AND TASTY

It is worth keeping a stash of different flavoured pastes that you can easily find in the supermarket: think chipotle, jerk, curry, harissa, gochujang and the like. These can be used very quickly in pasta dishes, fried rice and noodle dishes, and to add flavour to grilled meat and fish with ease. Quick and easy doesn't have to mean boring.

THE EXPEDIENT INGREDIENT

Don't be ashamed to make the most of supermarket jars of convenience, like grated ginger, garlic or chilli purées. This can be a point of contention, but comes down to personal priorities and preference. In all honesty, I never use garlic purée (see above) and the same applies to garlic granules or powder as the flavour is quite different to raw garlic and lacks that pungent pow; however, garlic granules are absolutely made for convenient flavour-boosting in other ways, particularly when mixed with other spices and herbs. Conversely, ginger purée is something I do use often as its convenience far outweighs all that peeling and grating. You will see though, that there are a couple of recipes where I call for fresh ginger; this is purely where the pungency of fresh ginger is important to the flavour profile of that dish.

Quite often when a recipe calls for diced peppers, I reach for jarred peppers and snip them straight into my dish. It is an especially great trick when a recipe calls for roasting or charring a pepper first.

There's always a time and a place for bags of pre-grated cheese. Ok, I won't be serving this on a cheeseboard anytime soon, but it can often be cheaper than a block of cheese and you can sometimes find bags of mixed Cheddar and mozzarella (ideal for quick pizzas), or pre-grated Gruyère or Emmental – mix with grated Cheddar for toasties to give that hint of nuttiness and the lovely sought-after cheesy pull.

Tomato ketchup can do the job of vinegar, sugar and tomato paste and you'll see it crop up in a few of my recipes. So get involved with a bottle of the finest red stuff. It doesn't have to be of artisan quality, but should ideally be a decent brand that is not too vinegary or sweet. It can really help to balance dishes and impart depth of flavour in the easiest way possible.

7

ONE-POT PERFECTION AND ONE-TIN TERRIFICNESS

Just like your freezer, the oven is another heaven-sent resource that we all have. By being clever with ingredients and dishes you can create an all-in-one meal where the ingredients go into one pot or roasting tin and then on to the hob or into the oven. This is the bung-it-all-in approach, no thought needed, the oven (or hob) left to work its magic while you get on with your day, then pop by half an hour or so later to a meal that has taken care of itself. Think pasta bakes, rice-based dishes (using previously frozen, or ready cooked rice), casseroles and stews.

8

BE EXTRA

Ok, so this is all about elevating very, very simple recipes into something a little special. Keep your kitchen stocked with nuts and seeds (perfect for toasting and sprinkling), chillies and spring onions for snipping over, oils and sauces for drizzling, cheeses for crumbling or grating. By adding all these different colours, textures and flavours to a finished dish you take a humble, simple but delicious meal and really lift it to another level.

9

SWAPSIE-SWAPSIE/SAD VEG

Don't have peas? Sub in another vegetable, like sweetcorn. Don't be scared to add in that odd sad end of carrot, or use frozen veg in recipes like stews, curries and casseroles – these are dishes that are absolutely perfect for avoiding waste. This doesn't just apply to veg; no prawns? Try thin strips of chicken!

10

WEIGHING IT ALL UP

One of my biggest bugbears is having to get out my scales to weigh out ingredients. It can be such a faff and naturally extends the whole cooking process. I know a lot of the time it can come down to confidence, but sometimes you don't need to be tied to the scales. Have the courage to throw in what you think looks right; for example, if a recipe for four calls for 300g frozen peas, rather than weighing it all out, visualise four portions as you take handfuls from the bag. Of course, there are situations where this doesn't work, for example in baking, where measurements do need to be exact to work.

MUST-HAVE / EASY KITCHEN TOOLS

When it comes to kitchen tools, I have done all the hard work (experimenting with what works) so you don't have to. Of course, you can go all out with various state-of-the-art gadgets to make things even easier, but you really don't need to. Here are the five clever tools I think every kitchen should have, to make light work of prep.

1 Sharp, sturdy pair of kitchen scissors (replaces the need for a knife in many a situation).

2 Vegetable peeler (easily ribbons carrots, cucumbers, courgettes and cabbage).

3 Garlic crusher (who needs to chop garlic?).

4 A decent grater. I love a Microplane for finely grating ingredients like fresh ginger and citrus zest. But it's also important to have a box grater, for coarsely grating carrots and cheese etc.

5 A simple blender or food processor. I have also bought a very small mini food chopper for chopping onions, making quick pastes and the like – it involves very little to put together and is easy to wash up, so I don't have to always get out my shiny, big, bells and whistles one! It is worth investing in both if you can. They'll become indispensable for blitzing sauces and chopping onions, herbs and other ingredients.

QUICK MEALS / IN MOMENTS

Here are some ingredients you should *always* have stocked in your kitchen so you can throw together meals in moments. Learn to mix and match the ingredients suggested here and with the confidence you will gain from following the recipes in the book, you will soon be creating quick dishes with a range of different flavour profiles.

Protein

Tinned pulses (chickpeas, beans and lentils), frozen thin strips of chicken, sausages, frozen fish, frozen gyoza.

Flavour

Pastes (curry, jerk, harissa, gochujang etc), spice mixes, ready-made sauces, soups and pesto.

Extras

Fresh herbs, chillies, spring onions, citrus wedges, nuts and seeds.

Vegetables

Frozen mixed vegetables, fresh vegetables in your fridge, tinned veg, ready-to-go soups.

Carbs

Potatoes, rice (I always have cooked rice in my freezer – it's far quicker to defrost than cooking from scratch!), pasta, couscous, frozen ready-to-roll pastry.

A FEW NOTES ABOUT / THE RECIPES

Cooking is not an exact science. That is to say, don't fret if you find you have a little less or a little more of an ingredient than the recipe prescribes. The odd discrepancy will not make a difference. (This is a rule for life by the way.) Unless you are baking and it states otherwise . . .

Throughout these recipes I refer to a mug as a measurement. This is to avoid having to get the scales out for every recipe. To find your perfect measuring mug, grab one that is full to the brim when you pour in about 300ml (or when you pop it on your scales, set to zero and top up with water, it weighs about 300g). Where helpful, I have left some weight measurements in, so you can use

those too, if you prefer. But really, the idea is to encourage you to feel brave enough to throw in odds and ends throughout your cooking and to judge quantities by eye, without always having to rely on specific gram for gram measurements. Of course, where baking is involved, the measurements do need to be a bit more precise there, so I have given weight, just in case it makes you feel a little more confident to have.

Many of the recipes have *Elevate it* suggestions, and these are purely suggestions. The dish will taste great without these additional elements, but should you wish to finish your dish by topping or sprinkling with any or all of these elements it will take it to the next level in terms of looks, flavour, texture and fun.

Wherever I suggest snipping an ingredient, that means with kitchen scissors, but if you prefer, feel free to chop with a knife instead.

All onions are assumed peeled, unless otherwise stated. If you are using ready-diced onions, ½ mug will roughly be equivalent to 1 large onion and ⅓ mug to 1 small onion.Seasoning is ideally with sea salt flakes and freshly ground black pepper.

Where I refer to a stock cube, please feel free to interchange with stock pots.

Butter can be unsalted or salted, unless otherwise stated. Whichever you choose will affect how much seasoning you need to add, but you will taste this in your dishes.

Vegetable, rapeseed, sunflower and olive oil can be used interchangeably, unless otherwise stated. It is really important to use the stated oil though when it comes to frying as some oils have a lower smoke point that can leave a burnt, bitter taste across your fried goods.

Feel free to use Grana Padano instead of Parmesan; it is a less expensive Italian hard cheese that can give similar results.

Flour and cheese in mugs is unpacked, unless stated otherwise. (By packed, I mean compacted down into the mug.)

When filling mugs with veg, squish them in, or try to get the most amount in as possible, unless otherwise stated.

THE SYMBOLS

 HANDS-ON TIME
This shows at a glance how much hands-on prep and cooking time is required. Freezing, chilling and marinating time isn't included

 ONE POT
Recipes that only require one receptacle for cooking

 FREEZER-FRIENDLY SYMBOL
Suitable for freezing

 VEGETARIAN
Does what it says on the tin

 VEGAN
Suitable for vegans

 VEGETARIAN OPTION
These recipes are easily made vegetarian following the tips

 VEGAN OPTION
These recipes are easily made vegan following the tips

1

FEASTS IN
A FLASH

DINNERS IN
UNDER 30 MINUTES

Truly flavoursome flashiness on your table in less than 30 minutes from first snip.

NEARLY NUMBING NOODLES

250g packet of mushrooms (you can use less), torn

2 pak choi, leaves separated (or a small bag of spinach)

300g cooked egg noodles (or straight-to-wok noodles)

FOR THE NEARLY NUMBING SAUCE

2 tbsp sesame oil (or vegetable oil)

3 spring onions, snipped

3 garlic cloves, crushed

1 heaped tbsp ginger purée

2 tbsp Sichuan peppercorns, ground into a coarse powder*

3 heaped tbsp peanut butter

3 heaped tbsp Chinese-style chilli oil

½ veg (or chicken) stock cube, well crumbled

* use a pestle and mortar, spice grinder or mini food processor

Who doesn't love slurping on oodles of juicy noodles (minus the inevitable chilli splash in the eye situation)? I have always been a fan of the numbing effects of a good Dan Dan noodle, usually when made with minced pork and so much flavour it makes you jump out of your seat. This vegetarian version is ready in a snip of the time and only uses one pot (hurrah for ready-cooked noodles!) but still has all the oomph of tingling deliciousness. It is worth keeping sesame oil and chilli oil in your store cupboard as they are instant flavour boosters!

1. Start with the sauce. Heat the oil in a large wok or frying pan with a lid over a medium-high heat. Stir in the spring onions, garlic, ginger and Sichuan pepper and fry for a couple of minutes until the aromas are released. Stir in the peanut butter, chili oil, stock cube and 200ml boiling water and keep stirring until the sauce is well combined.
2. Add the mushrooms and pak choi, reduce the heat to a low simmer, pop the lid on and soften the veg for about 5 minutes. (If you are using spinach instead of pak choi, add to the pan for the last minute, just to wilt through.)
3. Stir through the cooked noodles, season to taste and enjoy.

ELEVATE IT:
Add sliced chillies, sesame seeds or coriander sprigs.

GO VEGAN:
Swap the egg noodles for rice noodles or other vegan noodles.

NO WASTE – FRIDGE FORAGE:
Perfect for mushrooms, pak choi or spinach that need using up NOW.

BUFFALO ROAST CAULI 'POTATO' SALAD

 SERVES 4 25 MIN V VE

1 small cauliflower, broken into small florets

1 tbsp olive oil

500g packet of gnocchi

2 celery sticks, finely snipped

3 spring onions, finely snipped

1 small block of blue cheese (150g), crumbled

4 tbsp mayonnaise

4 tbsp soured cream

1 small garlic clove, grated

2 tbsp hot sauce (I like Frank's)

Green salad, to serve

I have a thing for buffalo chicken wings and potato salad, so I thought why not combine the two? Et voila, a beautiful Frankenstein of a dish. Yes, there is no potato in its usual form, but what a godsend gnocchi is for a quick carb fix! There's no chicken in this either, but it's a great way to squeeze some cauliflower into your diet. It is quite rich, so you won't need a lot.

1. Preheat the oven to 200°C/180°C fan/Gas Mark 6. Pop the cauliflower onto a large baking tray, toss with the oil and sprinkle over a little seasoning then roast in the oven for about 20 minutes, or until the cauli is cooked through and tender, with a little crispness and colour forming on the edges. Give it a stir halfway through the cooking time.
2. In the meantime, cook the gnocchi according to the packet instructions, then allow to cool for a couple of minutes.
3. Pop the gnocchi and cauliflower into a large bowl, then add the celery, spring onions and crumbled cheese.
4. Mix together the mayonnaise, soured cream, garlic and hot sauce and toss this through the bowl of veg. Don't mix too much – you don't want it to be mushy. Enjoy immediately.

ELEVATE IT:
Sprinkle over crispy bacon bits.

NO WASTE – FRIDGE FORAGE:
Perfect for slightly soft cauliflower.

GO VEGAN:
Substitute the blue cheese, mayo and soured cream for vegan alternatives.

FIRECRACKER QUESADILLAS

SERVES 2-4 · 20 MIN · V · VE

14 spring onions, white bulbs discarded

1 jarred red pepper

1–2 tbsp jarred jalapeño peppers

1 tbsp olive oil (or vegetable oil)

1 tsp ground cumin

1 tsp paprika (smoked or sweet)

1 large tin of sweetcorn (about 300g), drained (or use 1 mug frozen sweetcorn)

400g tin of kidney or black beans, drained and roughly crushed with a fork

Juice of ½ lime

4 tortilla wraps

2 mugs of grated Cheddar cheese

FOR THE LIME SOURED CREAM

Zest of 1 lime and juice of ½

1 small pot of soured cream (150ml)

This is *the* *fridge forage* and *leftover*s template to end all templates. Throw in sad salad or leftover cooked meats, or you can tailor each quesadilla to any taste by simply leaving out or adding in an element. The lime soured cream is a perfect accompaniment, but you can serve with ready-made guac, or just mashed avocado. Do freeze a few for future fast food!

1. Pop the spring onions, red pepper and jalapeños in a sturdy mixing bowl (Pyrex or metal). Using a pizza cutter, go over and slice the ingredients a few times into smaller shreds and pieces.
2. Heat the oil in a large frying pan over a high heat. Tip the contents of the bowl into the pan, along with the cumin, paprika, sweetcorn, crushed beans, lime juice and a pinch of seasoning. Cook for 5 minutes, stirring regularly.
3. Make the lime soured cream by mixing the ingredients together, seasoning to taste.
4. Take a tortilla wrap and a sprinkle ¼ mug of the cheese over one half of the wrap, then layer on top a quarter of the sweetcorn and bean mixture, then finally layer over another ¼ mug of cheese. Carefully fold the bare half of the tortilla over the filling. Repeat with the remaining ingredients.
5. Place a dry frying pan over a high heat. Pop the filled quesadilla into the pan and cook for a couple of minutes on one side, pressing down with a spatula, then flip over carefully and cook for another minute or so on the other side until the cheese has melted. Remove from the heat, cut in half and enjoy immediately with the lime soured cream.

ELEVATE IT:
Add guacamole or avocado slices, coriander sprigs, chopped chillies.

GO VEGAN:
Substitute the Cheddar and soured cream for vegan alternatives.

NO WASTE – LOVE YOUR LEFTOVERS:
Use up leftover cooked shredded chicken, beef, pork or other cooked meat, or random charcuterie. Make with leftover roasted veg, like potatoes, carrots and red onions.

FOREST BOLOGNESE

3 tbsp dried mushrooms, e.g. porcini

2 tbsp olive oil

4 spring onions, snipped

3 garlic cloves, crushed

2 carrots, grated

½ bunch of basil, torn

1 tbsp dried oregano

About 400g packet of mushrooms, torn finely

400g tin of chopped tomatoes

1 heaped tbsp tomato ketchup

1 tsp chilli flakes

100g walnuts, roughly crushed

1 veg stock cube, crumbled

Cooked spaghetti, to serve

This is such a wonderful change from the beautiful beef stuff, so regardless of whether you are vegetarian or not, why not switch it up a little? The umami from the dried mushrooms works its magic across this Bolognese so you don't miss the meat and it's a great way to squeeze in the veg! You may not want to go back to the classic version . . .

1. Pop the dried mushrooms in a mug, pour over boiling water to cover and leave them to soak while you get on with the rest of the recipe.
2. Heat the oil in a large saucepan over a medium heat, add the spring onions, garlic, carrots, basil (keep a few leaves back to serve), the oregano and fresh mushrooms and cook for 10 minutes, stirring regularly, until the veg are soft.
3. Add the chopped tomatoes, ketchup, chilli flakes, soaked mushrooms (and their liquid), walnuts and crumbled stock cube. Bring to the boil then reduce the heat to low and cook until thickened and rich, about 20 minutes. Season to taste and serve with heaps of spaghetti, a few basil leaves and any other toppings you wish.

ELEVATE IT:
Add a slick of extra virgin olive oil or some grated Parmesan cheese (choose a vegan alternative to keep this vegan).

NO WASTE – FRIDGE FORAGE:
Perfect for using up wrinkled mushrooms and forgotten packets of basil.

HARISSA ROAST GNOCCHI BAKE

SERVES 4 · 30 MIN · V · VE

4 tbsp extra virgin olive oil

2 tbsp rose harissa paste

1 red onion, unpeeled, cut into 8 wedges

3 garlic cloves, unpeeled, smashed

2 mugs of cherry tomatoes (about 300g)

500g packet of gnocchi

½–1 small bag of rocket

½ packet of feta cheese, crumbled

Traybake heaven. By which I mean: throw ingredients into a baking dish, pop into the oven and let it do the hard work. The flavours work so well together and that little crispy gnocchi exterior is a joy to bite into. Midweek magic!

1. Preheat the oven to 240°C/220°C fan/Gas Mark 8.
2. In a large roasting in, mix together half the olive oil and half the harissa paste with the onion, garlic and tomatoes, along with a pinch of seasoning. Spread this out on one side of the roasting tin. On the other half of the roasting tin, mix together the gnocchi with the remaining olive oil and harissa paste. Pop into the oven and bake for 25–30 minutes until the gnocchi is crispy and golden and the tomatoes have softened a bit.
3. Toss the gnocchi through the softened veg, then add the rocket and crumbled feta. Season to taste and enjoy immediately.

ELEVATE IT:
Toss through basil leaves, black olives, pine nuts.

NO WASTE – FRIDGE FORAGE:
Perfect for using up sad tomatoes and a little less crisp rocket.

GO VEGAN:
Substitute the feta for a vegan alternative.

MEDITERRANEAN CHICKEN KEBABS

 SERVES 4 15 MIN

1 bag of Mediterranean Chicken Strippers (see page 188)

4–8 pitta breads, lightly toasted and opened into pockets (or 4 warmed flatbreads)

Mixed salad (shredded lettuce, sliced tomato and red onion)

Lemon wedges, for squeezing over

FOR THE TZATZIKI

½ cucumber, seeds scooped out with a spoon, coarsely grated

8 tbsp natural yoghurt (150g pot)

1 small garlic clove, crushed

½ packet of mint leaves, snipped

Do you ever panic when you see the words 'marinating' and 'overnight' in the same sentence? Don't . . . it is literally shoving ingredients into a bowl or bag and letting the fridge do the hard work and it's SO worthwhile, especially when it means that these perfect partner spices and herbs have time to work their magic. Panic. Over. This kebab is the gift that keeps on giving. Go to town with your choice of salad and accompaniments – I highly recommend Turkish pickles, or the cheeky cheat's jarred jalapeño peppers.

1. Grab a freezer bag of the Mediterranean Chicken Strippers from the freezer and cook in batches over a medium-high heat in a large frying pan, with a little oil. Make sure you don't overcrowd the pan. Fry until the chicken is cooked through and a little golden, then set aside on a plate.
2. Meanwhile, mix together the ingredients for the tzatziki and season to taste.
3. Drizzle the inside of each pitta with tzatziki, stuff the pockets with the salad and then pile in the Chicken Strippers along with any juices from the frying pan. Drizzle over extra tzatziki, squeeze over some lemon juice and enjoy.

ELEVATE IT:
Add coriander sprigs, a mix of pickles (ideally Turkish-style, or use jarred jalapeños), sriracha.

NO WASTE – FRIDGE FORAGE:
Perfect for SAD salad that's a little on the flat side; the combination of textures and the lemon juice will mask and revive it.

NO WASTE – LOVE YOUR LEFTOVERS:
Use up leftover cooked chicken, pork or lamb. Just pull or shred into large chunks, brush with the marinade and grill until charred and piping hot. Use up leftover roasted veg (think potatoes, carrots, aubergine or red onion). Brush in the marinade and grill or heat in the oven at 180°C/160°C fan/Gas Mark 4 until piping hot.

CHILLI CON SAUSAGE

SERVES 4 · 30 MIN · VE

2 tbsp olive oil (or vegetable oil)

4 spring onions, finely snipped

3 garlic cloves, crushed

1 large carrot, grated

2 jarred red peppers, torn into small shreds

1 tbsp ground cumin

1 tbsp paprika (smoked or sweet)

1 tbsp ground coriander

1 heaped tsp chilli powder

8 sausages, squeezed out of their cases

400g tin of chopped tomatoes

400g tin of kidney beans, drained

3 heaped tbsp ketchup

White rice or jacket potato, to serve

I'm not going to be winning any authenticity points here, but flavour points? This has to be a 10/10. A great reason to always have sausages in the freezer, this recipe is veg-packed and incredibly quick to make. Grating the carrot not only means no chopping, but it cooks quicker too! An absolute winner!

1. Heat the oil in a large saucepan over a medium heat, add the spring onions, garlic, carrot and peppers and soften for about 5 minutes, then add the cumin, paprika, coriander and chilli powder and stir until the aromas are released.
2. Add the sausage meat and brown all over, then add the chopped tomatoes, kidney beans, half a tin of water and the ketchup. Bring to the boil then reduce to a low simmer and cook, with the lid on, for about 20 minutes until thickened and cooked through.
3. Serve with rice, or over a jacket potato.

ELEVATE IT:
Add grated Cheddar, chopped coriander leaves, soured cream, jalapeños, tortilla chips.

GO VEGGIE OR VEGAN:
Substitute the sausages for a squidgy, squeezable plant-based alternative.

MEXICAN BRUNCH BURRITO

SERVES 4 · 30 MIN · V

2 tbsp olive oil (or vegetable oil)

1 onion, peeled and pulsed in a food processor until roughly chopped

2 jarred red peppers, pulled into slivers

2 garlic cloves, crushed

1 tbsp paprika (smoked or sweet)

1 tbsp ground cumin

½–1 tsp chilli powder

2 packets of diced chorizo (about 150g), or ½ ring of chorizo, snipped into 2-cm coins

400g tin of chopped tomatoes

4 eggs

4 tortilla wraps, warmed

This is essentially a Mexican-style shakshuka in a wrap and it makes an incredible brunch dish for a lazy, hungover weekend. Actually, it's pretty amazing as a weeknight meal too. I adore these sauce-based dishes as they are perfect for using up random bits of veg or salad. My husband has a thing for crispy-bottomed fried eggs, so often I will fry the eggs in a small frying pan instead of braising them in the sauce. Go to town with elevating it – in this case more is more!

1. Heat the oil in a large frying pan over a medium heat and fry the onion and peppers until golden and soft, about 10 minutes. Add the garlic, spices and chorizo and stir until the aromas hit you. Add the chopped tomatoes along with a pinch of seasoning and simmer over a medium heat until thick and rich, about 10 minutes.
2. Make 4 wells in the spicy sauce and break the eggs in. Cook until the egg whites are cooked through and the yolks are still runny.
3. Divide among the tortilla wraps, wrap up and eat with your hands!

ELEVATE IT:
Fill the tortilla wraps with refried beans, guacamole, grated Cheddar, soured cream, chopped coriander, jalapeño peppers.

NO WASTE – FRIDGE FORAGE:
Use up wilting or wrinkly veg like spinach, mushrooms, courgette or squash as well as wilty coriander – just add with the chopped tomatoes in step 1.

GO VEGGIE:
Just leave out the chorizo!

NO WASTE – LOVE YOUR LEFTOVERS:
Make with leftover cooked shredded chicken, pork or beef or charcuterie, or crushed roasted veg (potato, sweet potato, carrot, onion etc.). Throw the ingredients in with the tomatoes in step 1 and make sure it is piping hot before serving.

CAJUN HASH BENEDICT

SERVES 4 · 30 MIN · V

2 large sweet potatoes (unpeeled), halved and pulsed in a food processor until roughly chopped (or use a box grater)

2 heaped tbsp butter, plus extra if needed

1 large onion, peeled and blitzed in a food processor until roughly chopped

2 heaped tbsp jarred jalapeño peppers, drained

3 garlic cloves, crushed

1 heaped tbsp Cajun seasoning

120g packet of diced chorizo or ½ dry-cured chorizo ring, skin peeled off and crumbled

1 large handful of spinach

1 quantity of Hasty Hollandaise (see page 193), with 1 tsp Cajun seasoning

I just don't know where to begin with this beauty – I'm sure I don't need to say that it's not just for brunch! It has all the goodness you'd expect from a hash, with the added benefit of a foolproof hollandaise drizzle, all with a fiery Cajun twist. There are a few processes, but they are quick and so worthwhile. I blitz the sweet potato in a food processor to get a finer dice, almost halfway between diced and grated potato.

1. Parboil the pulsed sweet potatoes for 5 minutes, then drain and leave to steam-dry.
2. Pop the butter into a large frying pan over a medium heat. When the butter starts to foam and darken, add the onion and soften for 5 minutes, then add the jalapeños, garlic, Cajun seasoning and chorizo and cook for another 5 minutes, stirring often.
3. Add the sweet potato and stir to combine, then cook for 10–15 minutes until cooked through, squashing with a fish slice to allow a little golden crust to build up a little before flipping over and repeating. Add a little more butter if the pan is a bit dry.
4. Meanwhile, make the hollandaise following the instructions on page 193, adding Cajun seasoning. Keep warm until ready to serve.
5. Add the spinach to the hash and cook for another 5 minutes, stirring occasionally. Season to taste, then serve with the Hasty Hollandaise.

ELEVATE IT:
Top with fried eggs, parsley, fresh chilli.

NO WASTE – FRIDGE FORAGE:
Ideal for using up soggy spinach.

GO VEGGIE:
Swap the chorizo for vegetarian chorizo or other veg, like tomato and mushrooms.

KIND OF KEEMA LAMB PAU

 SERVES 4 30 MIN VE

1 tbsp butter

1 onion, peeled and quickly pulsed in a processor until roughly chopped

3 garlic cloves, crushed

2 tbsp ginger purée

1 tbsp ground cumin

1 tbsp garam masala

½–1 tsp chilli powder

3 heaped tbsp ketchup

400-500g packet of lamb mince

½ chicken or veg stock cube, crumbled

1 mug of frozen peas

4 toasted and buttered brioche burger buns (or use plain burger buns)

For Indian-spiced comfort, this one's for you! It has become a firm family fave in my household and for any lamb-naysayers out there . . . I promise you that this will turn you, the flavour creeping through this is utterly sublime. I recommend trying this in buttery brioche buns but you can enjoy with rice or naan if you prefer.

1. Heat the butter in a large saucepan over a high heat, then soften the onion with a pinch of salt, stirring often, for about 10 minutes until golden brown.
2. Add the garlic, ginger, spices and ketchup and fry, stirring continuously, until the aromas hit you. Add the mince and brown all over, then add the stock cube along with half a mug of boiling water and some seasoning. Reduce the heat to low and simmer for 15 minutes, stirring occasionally and adding the peas during the last few minutes, until warmed through. There shouldn't be much sauce.
3. Season to taste, then pile into the buttery toasted buns.

ELEVATE IT:
Add chopped coriander, sliced red onion, lime wedges, green chilli, raita.

GO VEGGIE OR VEGAN:
Substitute the lamb mince for a plant-based alternative and to make it vegan use oil instead of butter to fry the onion and a vegan burger bun.

CHORIZO & SEAFOOD 'PAELLA'

SERVES 4 · 15 MIN

2 tbsp olive oil

3 spring onions, snipped

2 large garlic cloves, crushed

1 tbsp smoked paprika

½ jar (about 450g) roasted red peppers, drained and torn into large strips

2 x 60g packets of diced chorizo, or ½ chorizo ring, snipped into 1-cm thick rounds

2 heaped tbsp tomato purée

2 x 250g pouches of microwave rice, cooked according to the packet instructions

½ chicken stock cube, crumbled

½ mug of black olives

½ mug of frozen peas, left to defrost at room temperature for a few minutes

About 500g packet of cooked frozen seafood (or use prawns, calamari or mussels)

Lemon wedges, to serve

This is the quick-fix, seaside dish you've been waiting for: all the flavours of paella but with microwaveable rice and frozen cooked seafood taking starring roles. The key is to cook it until the seafood is just heated through so it doesn't become tough. You can swap in cooked shredded chicken instead (or as well as!). Using ready-cooked ingredients will bring the time you are waiting to eat right down, putting a mid-week paella back on the menu!

1. Heat the oil in a large frying pan over a medium heat and cook the spring onions, garlic, paprika and peppers until the aromas are released. Add the chorizo and continue to cook until it releases its oil and begins to crisp up a little.
2. Add the tomato purée and the cooked rice to the pan and stir until the grains are well coated, then add ½ mug of boiling water, the crumbled stock cube, olives, peas and seafood along with a pinch of seasoning. Pop the lid on, reduce the heat to low and cook until the seafood is hot through and the water has been absorbed by the rice, about 5 minutes.
3. Serve with lemon wedges for squeezing over.

ELEVATE IT:
Scatter over parsley leaves and chopped chillies before serving.

NO WASTE – LOVE YOUR LEFTOVERS:
Perfect for throwing in cooked veg like carrot, sweetcorn, or small broccoli florets. Just add in step 2, along with the peas.

CHEATBALLS

SERVES 4 · 30 MIN · V

1 onion, peeled

3 garlic cloves

2 x 400g tins of lentils (green or brown), drained

6 heaped tbsp breadcrumbs

2 heaped tbsp ketchup

2 tsp dried oregano

2 large eggs

Olive oil (or vegetable oil), for frying

TO SERVE

Cooked spaghetti

Large jar of ready-made tomato pasta sauce (or make your own, see page 186)

This store cupboard dinner can be thrown together with such a simple selection of ingredients. It really makes a delicious meat-free 'meatball' to pile on top of spaghetti, although you could also go rogue by serving with mashed or roast potatoes or stuff into a roll with mozzarella to make a meatball sandwich.

1. Preheat the oven to 190°C/170°C fan/Gas Mark 5.
2. In a food processor, roughly pulse the onion and garlic for a few minutes until finely chopped, then mix in the remaining ingredients along with a pinch of seasoning.
3. Divide the mixture into 20–24 balls, then pop them onto a greased baking tray and then into the oven for about 20 minutes until firm.
4. Heat a few tablespoons of oil in a large frying pan and brown the cheatballs on all sides, in batches. Place on a plate lined with kitchen paper to soak up the excess oil. Serve piled high on a bowl of spaghetti with tomato sauce.

NO WASTE – FRIDGE FORAGE:
Use up sad and wilting veg like spinach, mushrooms or courgettes: just add in when you are rough pulsing the onion but try not to add more than a handful of veg as the cheatballs may become too soggy. Balance the addition of veg by adding a little more ketchup, oregano, seasoning and breadcrumbs so the mixture comes together like meatballs.

SAUSAGE & MUSHROOM RAGU

SERVES 4 · 30 MIN · VE

2 tbsp olive oil

1 large carrot, grated

3 spring onions, finely snipped

2 garlic cloves, crushed

1 heaped mug of mushrooms, roughly torn

1 tsp dried oregano

1 tsp fennel seeds

6 pork sausages, squeezed out of their cases

400g tin of chopped tomatoes

1 heaped tbsp tomato ketchup

1 tsp chilli flakes

Cooked pasta, mashed potato or couscous, to serve

Looking for a low-hassle Bolognese? If you fancy a change then this ragu is just the thing for you: it's quick and made from kitchen basics and the sausages are a pleasant alternative to the classic minced beef. Why ketchup? It's the perfect kitchen classic, doing the job of tomato flavour, acid and sugar – 3 in 1! Perfect to flood pasta, jacket potatoes and couscous.

1. In a medium-sized saucepan, heat the oil and soften the grated carrot, spring onions, garlic, mushrooms, oregano, fennel seeds and a pinch of salt for about 5 minutes.
2. Add the sausage meat, brown all over, then add the chopped tomatoes and ketchup, along with the chilli flakes and a pinch of seasoning. Reduce the heat, pop the lid on and cook until thick and rich and the sausage is cooked through, about 20 minutes, stirring now and again.
3. Season to taste and serve over buttery mashed potato, pasta or couscous.

ELEVATE IT:
Add grated Parmesan cheese, fresh basil.

NO WASTE – FRIDGE FORAGE:
Perfect for using up wrinkly mushroom.

GO VEGGIE OR VEGAN:
Substitute the sausages for veggie or vegan sausages, ensuring they are squidgy and not firm, so that you can squash them down into a ragu.

INSIDE OUT CHICKEN KYIV

 SERVES **4**   **25 MIN**

4 skinless chicken breasts

12 heaped tbsp breadcrumbs (panko gives a crunchier crumb, but basic works well too)

Vegetable oil, for frying

Buttery mashed potato and greens, to serve

FOR THE GARLIC BUTTER

5 heaped tbsp butter

1 garlic clove, crushed

2 tbsp finely snipped parsley (¼ bunch)

Pinch of chilli flakes

Ok, for all you purists, this isn't really and truly a Kyiv, but to all intents and purposes a forkful of it delivers the same punch of flavours and bite without any messy breadcrumbing production line or chicken stuffing. This technique for instant crumbing is intended for chicken to be cooked soon, rather than to be frozen.

1. Pop a chicken breast on a chopping board and place an A4-size sheet of parchment paper (or a silicone sheet) on top. Flatten the breast by pounding it with a rolling pin. Sprinkle a little seasoning on both sides. Firmly press the breadcrumbs into the chicken with your hand, then gently flip over and press more onto the other side. Set aside on a plate or tray. Repeat with the other chicken breasts.

2. In a large frying pan, pour enough oil to cover the base of the pan and place over a medium-high heat. Carefully place the chicken into the pan (you may need to do this in batches) and fry until golden on both sides and cooked through, about 3 minutes on each side. Set aside on a plate lined with kitchen paper.

3. Meanwhile, make the garlic butter. Pop the butter, garlic, parsley and chilli flakes into a small saucepan with a little pinch of seasoning and place over a low heat until the butter has melted and the aromas hit you. Set aside.

4. Serve the chicken generously drizzled with the garlic butter and alongside buttery mashed potato and greens.

TIP:
Try this crumbing technique with fish fillets or goujons.

NO WASTE – FRIDGE FORAGE:
Perfect to use up wilting parsley.

MICRO ZAP BIBIMBAP

SERVES 2 · 15 MIN · V

2 minute (thin-cut/bavette) beef steaks, snipped into thin strips

2 garlic cloves, crushed

2 tbsp white wine/cider vinegar

2 heaped tbsp gochujang paste, plus 1 tbsp thinned to drizzle consistency with hot water

2 tbsp soy sauce

3 tbsp toasted sesame oil

1 packet of mixed stir-fry veg (about 300g)

1 x 250g pouch of microwave basmati (or long-grain) rice, cooked according to the packet instructions

2 eggs

Thank goodness for modern convenience foods like microwaveable rice and ready-to-cook mixed veg! They quite often come in cheaper than buying all the different veg individually, plus the time saved on all that chopping makes it worthwhile. Minute steak is perfect for midweek meals as it's cooked in moments (it also defrosts very quickly) and is cost-effective, so it's always worth having a pack in your freezer.

1. Mix the steak strips with the garlic, vinegar, the 2 tablespoons of gochujang and the soy sauce in a small bowl, along with a pinch of seasoning.
2. In the meantime, heat 2 tablespoons of the sesame oil a large frying pan or wok over a high heat, add the steak, along with any marinade, and fry quickly until well browned on the outside. Pop on to a plate and cover with foil to rest.
3. Add a splash of sesame oil to the hot pan, add the stir-fry veg and cook, stirring often, for about 3 minutes, then set aside in serving bowls, alongside the cooked rice.
4. Reduce the heat to medium-high, wipe the pan with kitchen paper, add a splash more oil, then crack in the eggs and fry until the white is cooked but the yolk is still runny.
5. Add the beef strips to the bowls, top each with an egg and a drizzle of the watered down gochujang and elevate it!

ELEVATE IT:
Add toasted sesame seeds, kimchi, sriracha.

GO VEGGIE:
Leave out the steak, or swap with firm tofu and fry until golden.

2

MEALS NEEDING MORE

DINNERS OVER 30 MINUTES

Still cleverly simple stunners with minimal prep, but may require a little more hot lovin' from the hob or oven.

Spaghetti Meatballs Traybake 64

Crispy Tofu Asian Loaded Fries 66

Chicken Cobbler 68

Hoisin Mushroom Pancakes 70

Corn Dumpling Soup 71

Chilli Thyme Roasted Tomatoes & Feta 72

Curried Fish Jackets 74

Anytime Breakfast Smash 75

Mumbai Roasted Potato 76

Lemon Olive Oil Lamb & Two Veg 78

One-tin Spring Roast Chicken 80

Veg Hero Burgers 81

Picnic Loaf 82

Fish (& Chip) Cakes 84

Melting Beef Pot 85

SPAGHETTI MEATBALLS TRAYBAKE

 SERVES 4 55 MIN

3 tbsp olive oil

16–20 ready-made meatballs (uncooked)

½ onion, peeled and grated

1 large garlic clove, crushed

1 large jar (about 400g) of marinara or tomato sauce (or make your own, see page 186)

1 heaped tbsp tomato ketchup

3½ x 10p-sized rounds of dried uncooked spaghetti (about 400g)

1 veg stock cube, crumbled

1 mug of grated Cheddar or Parmesan cheese

Regularly requested by my boys, spaghetti and meatballs is family food heaven. This richer, meatier-tasting version takes out the faff by throwing everything into one dish (a win on the washing-up front!) and into the magic oven; there's no pre-cooking of the pasta required (the spaghetti is thin enough to cook quickly) and there's no separate heating of sauce. Ready-made meatballs – another faff-reducing shortcut – are easily found in the supermarket, so keep some stashed in your freezer at all times, ready to go.

1. Preheat the oven to 200°C/180°C fan/Gas Mark 6.
2. Heat 2 tablespoons of the oil in a deep-sided ovenproof pan over a medium-high heat, throw in the meatballs and onion and brown all over (you may need to do this in batches).
3. Add the garlic, tomato sauce, ketchup, remaining tablespoon of oil and the spaghetti (you may need to break it in half to fit into the pan). Add a pinch of seasoning, the crumbled stock cube and 2 mugs of boiling water and give everything a good stir.
4. Pop the lid on (or cover with foil) and bake in the oven for 30–40 minutes, stirring after 15 minutes, until the spaghetti and meatballs are cooked through and most of the liquid is absorbed, leaving just a little sauce. Top with the grated cheese and serve immediately.

ELEVATE IT:
Scatter basil leaves over the top to serve.

NO WASTE – FRIDGE FORAGE:
Perfect for throwing in wrinkly veg like carrot, sweetcorn, broccoli or mushrooms. Just add in step 4.

CRISPY TOFU ASIAN LOADED FRIES

SERVES 4 · 35 MIN · VE

400–500g frozen oven fries, cooked according to the packet instructions (I love sweet potato fries, but really any will do)

1 tbsp Chinese five-spice

1 tbsp sesame oil

FOR THE CRISPY TOFU

3 tbsp cornflour

1 tsp garlic granules

½ tsp chilli powder

400g block of firm tofu, drained, patted dry with kitchen paper and cut into 1-cm cubes

Vegetable oil, for shallow-frying

FOR THE ASIAN 'LOADING'

Generous squeezes of mayonnaise (VE: make sure it's a vegan version)

Generous squeeze of sriracha

Generous squeeze of hoisin sauce

4 spring onions, finely snipped

2 tbsp snipped coriander leaves

Often called 'dirty fries', loaded fries are potatoes living their best life. This is a feast for the senses and the combination of flavour and crunch is heavenly. While the spiced oven fries are baking away, the tofu is easily cooked to crispy perfection with a ton of flavour. Then the fun begins: loading it with everything but the kitchen sink.

1. Preheat the oven according to the oven fries packet instructions. Tip the frozen fries onto a large baking tray and sprinkle over the five-spice along with a pinch of sea salt and black pepper. Drizzle over the sesame oil, toss together to coat and spread out in a single layer (you may need to use two trays). Pop into the oven and cook until cooked through and crisp and golden. Set aside for a couple minutes.

2. Meanwhile, for the crispy tofu, mix the cornflour, garlic granules, chilli powder, and a pinch of salt and pepper in a bowl. Add the cubed tofu and toss to combine.

3. Pour enough vegetable oil into a large frying pan so it completely covers the base and place over a medium-high heat. Set a plate lined with kitchen paper nearby. Fry the tofu for about 10–15 minutes, turning on all sides until golden and crunchy all over, then remove with a slotted spoon and pop onto the lined plate.

4. To plate up, pop the fries on to a large plate and stud with the tofu. Generously (and I mean go OTT) squiggle over the sauces, then sprinkle over the spring onions and coriander leaves and enjoy immediately.

ELEVATE IT:
Add thinly sliced radishes, finely chopped peanuts, toasted sesame seeds, lime wedges.

CHICKEN COBBLER

SERVES 4 · 45 MIN · V

2 tbsp olive oil

2 spring onions

3 garlic cloves, crushed

12 baby carrots (or 3 medium carrots, quartered)

1 tbsp dried thyme

1½–2 mugs of frozen chicken strips (or use 6 skinless thigh fillets/3 breasts, snipped into bite-size chunks or strips)

1 tbsp flour (self-raising or plain)

1 chicken or veg stock cube, crumbled

½ mug of frozen peas

5 tbsp double cream

FOR THE TOPPING

1 mug of plain flour (about 180g)

1 tsp baking powder

1 egg, beaten

2 heaped tbsp butter, melted

5 tbsp milk

I enjoy the word 'cobbler' as much as the next person. Lovely, golden scone-like clouds placed atop a chicken and veg casserole. Doesn't that sound heavenly? If you love a chicken pot pie, give this one a try – using clever shortcuts like baby carrots and our freezer stash of frozen Chicken Strippers (see page 188) it's hardly any effort and is a real winner with the kids too. You can also freeze the filling!

1. Preheat the oven to 220°C/200°C fan/Gas Mark 7. Heat the oil in a large casserole or ovenproof dish over a medium heat. Add the spring onions, garlic, carrots and thyme and cook for about 5 minutes. Add the chicken and brown all over.
2. Add the flour and stir until cooked, then stir in the stock cube, 1 mug (300ml) boiling water, the peas, double cream and a generous pinch of seasoning. Bring up to the boil then reduce the heat and simmer for about 5 minutes while you make the cobbler topping.
3. Mix together the flour, baking powder, egg, butter and milk with a pinch of salt. Divide the dough into 8–10 balls (to cover the top of the casserole) and press to make rough, small, palm-sized circles. Top the chicken casserole with the scone circles, brush them with a little milk and pop into the oven for 25–30 minutes, or until the cobbler is cooked and golden.

GO VEGGIE:
Just leave out the chicken and add extra veg, like sweetcorn, mushrooms and diced potatoes.

NO WASTE – FRIDGE FORAGE:
Use up forgotten veg – throw in that half tin of sweetcorn that never got used, or those broccoli florets at the back of your fridge in step 2 with the peas.

HOISIN MUSHROOM PANCAKES

SERVES 4 | 35 MIN | VE

2 x 300g packets of mushrooms, torn into small shreds

2 tsp Chinese five-spice

2 tsp sugar

4 tbsp sesame oil

6 heaped tbsp hoisin sauce, plus extra to serve

12–16 Chinese pancakes

6 spring onions, snipped into thin rounds, bulb discarded

1 cucumber, halved lengthways, deseeded with a spoon and sliced into half-moons

My boys love a good duck pancake. This mushroom version is ready in a snip of the time and it is great if you want a night off meat – it also tastes blummin' fantastic. I am very lucky to live close to a Chinese supermarket so I buy my pancakes in bulk (like, 100 at a time!) and then freeze them, so we can reach for this recipe at any moment, although they are now relatively easy to come by in a supermarket.

1. Preheat the oven to 200°C/180°C fan/Gas Mark 6.
2. Mix the shredded mushrooms with the Chinese five-spice, sugar and sesame oil. Spread the mushrooms out as flat as possible in a roasting tin, then pop into the oven for 30 minutes, giving a mix halfway through. Add the hoisin sauce, mix well, then pop under a hot grill for a couple minutes until the mushrooms start to caramelise and crisp up.
3. To serve, spread the pancakes with a little more hoisin sauce and top with the mushrooms, spring onions and cucumber. Wrap and eat immediately.

ELEVATE IT:
Sprinkle over toasted sesame seeds and/or chopped chillies before wrapping.

NO WASTE – FRIDGE FORAGE:
Perfect for using up forgotten packets of wrinkly mushrooms.

CORN DUMPLING SOUP

 SERVES 4 35 MIN VE

2 tbsp olive oil (or vegetable oil)

1 small packet of shredded ham hock or bacon lardons/pancetta (about 100g)

2 garlic cloves, crushed

3 spring onions, snipped

2 sprigs of thyme

Generous pinch of cayenne pepper

8 baby carrots (or 3 medium carrots, quartered)

4 corn cobettes (or 2 corn on the cobs, halved)

400ml tin of coconut milk

1 vegetable stock cube, crumbled

¾ mug of split lentils (about 200g)

400g packet of gnocchi

This is a quick riff on a popular Trinidadian street food. Usually made with salted pig tails and dumplings, I have taken some proper liberties here (or you might call it clever substitutions?) with ham hock and gnocchi replacing fiddly dumplings, and perfectly sized baby carrots and cobettes – and you know what? It tastes heavenly. Think less soup more stew here.

1. Heat the oil in a large, lidded casserole over a medium heat, add the ham hock and stir for a few seconds, then stir in the garlic, spring onions, thyme, cayenne pepper, carrots and corn cobettes. Cook for 5 minutes, stirring often.
2. Add the coconut milk, crumbled stock cube and lentils, along with 1½ tins (use the empty coconut milk tin) of boiling water (careful, it will be hot to hold!), along with a generous pinch of seasoning. Bring to the boil, then reduce the heat, pop the lid on and simmer until the lentils are soft, about 25 minutes. Stir often, adding the gnocchi for the last 5 minutes. Give everything a good stir, then enjoy.

ELEVATE IT:
Add chopped coriander, chopped chillies, chopped chives.

GO VEGAN:
Leave out the ham hock or bacon.

NO WASTE – FRIDGE FORAGE:
Use up sad veg like wrinkly carrots and feel free to throw in pumpkin and sweet potato if any needs using up.

CHILLI THYME ROASTED TOMATOES & FETA

 SERVES 4 35 MIN V VE

3 mugs of cherry tomatoes (or 500g packet of vine tomatoes, halved)

8 unpeeled garlic cloves, smashed

2 sprigs of thyme

½–1 tsp chilli flakes

8 tbsp extra virgin olive oil

1 block of feta cheese, roughly crumbled

Crusty warm bread or cooked pasta, to serve

Yes, this is inspired by the TikTok 'sensation' of 2021. But you know what, it really tastes quite lovely and is very simple to make. The addition of thyme and chilli give it a little level of sophistication. It may look watery, but give it all a good mix to bring everything together. It's so good, and not just for pasta!

1. Preheat the oven to 180°C/160°C fan/Gas Mark 4.
2. Mix all the ingredients in a roasting tin, along with a generous pinch of seasoning. Cover with foil and pop into the oven for about 30 minutes until the garlic is soft. Halfway through the cooking time give everything a mix and a squish with a fork and make sure the feta is coated in the tin juices. Remove the garlic skins.
3. Serve smooshed on crusty bread or mix through cooked pasta.

ELEVATE IT:
Sprinkle over chopped coriander leaves and toasted pine nuts, just before serving.

GO VEGAN:
Use vegan feta.

CURRIED FISH JACKETS

SERVES
4

40
MIN

4 baking potatoes

1 tbsp olive oil

2 spring onions, snipped

1 garlic clove, crushed

1 tsp mild curry powder

10 tbsp soured cream

1 tsp mustard (wholegrain or Dijon)

300g fish pie mix

½ mug of frozen peas

2 tbsp butter

½ mug of grated Cheddar cheese

These sweet, individually portioned fish pie(ish) jacket potatoes are the perfect no-effort freezer filler. If you can't find fish pie mix, just snip up a few different skinless fish fillets and add half a mug of raw prawns to make your own version. I love adding the curry powder for a little extra pizazz, but do feel free to leave it out.

1. Preheat the oven to 200°C/180°C fan/ Gas Mark 6. Give the potatoes a little prick with a fork and rub with oil and salt. Pop them into a microwave on high for 10–15 minutes until tender all around, turning over halfway. (Or, if you have more time, pop them on to a baking tray and bake until cooked through, about 1 hour.)
2. Allow the potatoes to cool, then cut them in half lengthways and scoop out the flesh into a bowl, leaving ½ cm still in the jacket to keep the potato skins sturdy.
3. While you wait for the potato to cool, heat the oil in a small pan over a medium heat, add the spring onions, garlic and curry powder and cook until softened and the aromas hit you. Add the soured cream, mustard, fish pie mix and peas, as well as a pinch of seasoning, and mix well. Turn off the heat.
4. Roughly mash the scooped-out potato with the butter, cheese and a pinch of salt and pepper.
5. Divide the fish pie mix between the skins, spoon over the seasoned mash and pop back into the oven for 20–25 minutes until the fish is cooked through. Finish under a hot grill until golden and bubbling, if you like.

ANYTIME BREAKFAST SMASH

SERVES 4 · 35 MIN · V

1 tbsp vegetable oil or olive oil

1 packet (about 180g) of lardons (or 6 rashers of streaky bacon, snipped or chopped into small pieces)

2 heaped tbsp butter

1 onion, peeled and quickly pulsed in a processor until roughly chopped

4 sausages, skinned and broken into large chunks

8 cherry tomatoes

1 mug of mushrooms, roughly torn

1 x 500g bag of baby new/miniature potatoes, boiled until tender, about 10 minutes

4 large eggs

Yes. This is what I'm talking about: fry-up meets a hash. The resulting dish is a beauty. This is a great canvas for any sad veg and salad that probably wouldn't work in a fresh dish; like a handful of spinach that needs using up.

1. Heat the oil in a large frying pan over a medium heat, then add the lardons and fry until crisp, about 5 minutes. Remove with a slotted spoon and set aside on a plate lined with kitchen paper.
2. Melt the butter in the same pan over a medium-high heat, then add the onion, sausage, tomatoes (piercing and squashing them with a fork) and mushrooms to the pan, along with some seasoning. Cook, stirring occasionally, for about 5 minutes.
3. Add the potatoes, squashing them with a potato masher or wooden spoon and cook for another 10–12 minutes until the potato gets a little crispy and charred, the onion is soft and golden and the sausage is cooked through.
4. Sprinkle over the crispy lardons. Reduce the heat to medium and make 4 wells in the hash, then break in the eggs, pop the lid on and cook until the whites are just cooked and the yolk is still runny. Season to taste and enjoy.

ELEVATE IT:
Top with chopped chillies, douses of Tabasco or other hot sauce.

NO WASTE – FRIDGE FORAGE:
Perfect for using up forgotten, soft veg like tomatoes, spinach or mushrooms.

GO VEGGIE:
Swap the bacon and sausages for veggie alternatives.

TIP:
I've stuck with an onion here, rather than the more snippable spring onion. Caramelisation is key to the flavour profile in this dish and you can only get this with onion, so take the extra effort here if you can!

MUMBAI ROASTED POTATO

SERVES 4 · 45 MIN · VE

800g bag of new/baby potatoes

4 tbsp olive oil or vegetable oil

2 tbsp ground cumin

2 tbsp garam masala

2 tsp ginger paste

4 unpeeled garlic cloves, smashed

FOR THE TAMARIND SAUCE

6 tbsp tamarind paste

Juice of 1 lime

1 tsp caster sugar

FOR THE FRESH 'CHUTNEY'

½ red onion, peeled and pulsed in a food processor until finely chopped

1–2 bird's-eye chillies, thinly snipped

¼ bunch of coriander, roughly snipped

10 mint leaves, roughly snipped

6 cherry or small vine tomatoes, halved

Taking inspiration from a few of my favourite Mumbai street foods, this mish-mash combo of spice-roasted potatoes with the deconstructed components of the chutney freshly scattered over and the tangy tamarind lime drizzle is a feast for the senses. Definitely worth elevating, especially with Bombay Mix for a fun textural contrast.

1. Preheat the oven to 200°C/180°C fan/Gas Mark 6.
2. Cook the potatoes in a saucepan of boiling salted water for 10 minutes, then drain and pop into a large roasting tin. Use a potato masher or fork to crush the potatoes, then drizzle over the oil, cumin, garam masala, ginger paste, garlic cloves and a generous pinch of seasoning. Gently toss the potatoes through the mixture and pop into the oven for about 20–30 minutes until golden and crispy.
3. Mix together the tamarind paste, lime juice and sugar and season to taste. Drizzle this over the potatoes, then scatter over all the 'chutney' ingredients and enjoy immediately.

ELEVATE IT:
Before serving, top with drizzles of yoghurt, pomegranate seeds, Bombay mix.

LEMON OLIVE OIL LAMB & TWO VEG

SERVES 4 · 4 HRS

6 baby onions

500–700g bag of baby new/miniature potatoes

1.5kg shoulder or leg of lamb, ideally bone-in

3 tbsp olive oil

Zest and juice of 1 lemon

1 whole head of garlic, unpeeled cloves separated and smashed

2 sprigs of rosemary, broken into smaller sprigs

1 packet of long-stem broccoli (like Tenderstem)

Mint sauce, to serve

I absolutely love this dish; it reminds me of that little piece of Greek heaven that is kleftiko. The lamb is achingly tender and falls apart on top of veg that has absorbed all the lamb juices. It really is a crowd-pleaser and looks stunning brought to the table straight from the oven. If you haven't got baby onions, go for the smallest shallots you can find (or simply quarter larger onions).

1. Preheat the oven to 150°C/130°C fan/Gas Mark 2.
2. Pop the onions and potatoes into a large, deep-sided roasting tin. Slash the lamb all over and place on top, then rub the lamb with the olive oil and lemon zest and juice. Push in to the slashes as many of the smashed garlic cloves and rosemary sprigs as you can – don't worry if some fall to the bottom of the pan – and then sprinkle over a little seasoning.
3. Loosely cover the roasting tin with foil, leaving enough room to create a 'tent', then pop into the oven for about 3½ hours, basting now and again, until the meat easily falls off the bone when pulled with a fork. Remove the lamb from the tin, pop the foil over it and leave to rest.
4. Whack the heat up to 220°C/200°C/Gas Mark 7. Add the broccoli to the potatoes and onions in the roasting tin, give it all a stir and cook for 15–20 minutes until the potatoes are crispy and the broccoli is tender. Remove from the oven, pop the lamb back on top of the veg and pull the meat apart with forks, drizzling over the pan juices before serving.

NO WASTE – FRIDGE FORAGE:
Perfect for bendy broccoli or not quite-at-their-best baby potatoes.

ONE-TIN SPRING ROAST CHICKEN

SERVES 4 | 1 HR

8 baby onions (or 2 small onions, peeled and quartered)

6 unpeeled garlic cloves, smashed

1 lemon, quartered and pips removed

500g baby new potatoes

1 mug of frozen peas

1 heaped tbsp dried oregano

2 tbsp olive oil, plus extra for brushing

8 chicken pieces (thighs or drumsticks) bone-in and skin-on

½ stock cube, crumbled into ⅓ mug of hot water

Crusty bread, to serve

This is a stunner of a recipe, a sort of quick-fix, oven-does-the-work Sunday roast option. It has a kind of spring feel to it, but by using frozen peas, you can make this year round; just use another available baby or miniature potato.

1. Preheat the oven to 200°C/180°C fan/Gas Mark 6.
2. Put the onions, garlic, lemon quarters, potatoes, peas, oregano and olive oil into a large roasting tin, in a single layer if possible. Toss well to ensure the ingredients are coated, then add the chicken, skin-side up, and brush with the extra oil. Pour in the stock and season with salt and pepper. Cover with foil and bake for 30 minutes.
3. Remove the foil and bake for another 20–30 minutes until the chicken is cooked through and the juices run clear and the potato is soft.
4. Preheat the grill to high and pop the tin under the grill for a few minutes to crisp up the chicken skin. Serve straight away, with plenty of crusty bread to mop up the juices.

ELEVATE IT:
Add spears of asparagus in step 2 and serve scattered with chopped parsley.

VEG HERO BURGERS

MAKES 6 | 25 MINS + CHILLING | V | VE

3 tbsp vegetable oil

2 garlic cloves, crushed

4 spring onions, finely snipped

1 courgette (about 200g), coarsely grated (or use a food processor)

2 large carrots, coarsely grated (or use a food processor)

1 heaped mug of mushrooms (about 100g), torn as finely as possible

¼ bunch of parsley, finely snipped

1 mug of grated Cheddar cheese

10 heaped tbsp breadcrumbs

400g tin of chickpeas, drained* and roughly crushed with a fork

6 burger buns (I love brioche), toasted

* Save the chickpea water (aquafaba) to make Black Forest Mousse (see page 172), or Mayo for Morons (see page 192)

This is the one to fill you up on your five-a-day without even feeling it. It has been tried and tested on veg-dodgers and fussy eaters . . . they just can't resist this meaty (meatless) burger. The food processor can really be your best friend here to get the job done quickly, otherwise treat the veg grating as a mindful moment!

1. Heat 1 tablespoon of the oil in a frying pan over a medium heat and fry the garlic, spring onions, courgette, carrot, mushrooms and parsley with a pinch of seasoning for about 5 minutes until soft, stirring regularly. Set aside to cool.
2. Tip the veg into a bowl, add the cheese, breadcrumbs and chickpeas with a little seasoning and mix until well combined. Form into 6 burger-sized patties and chill for 30 minutes in the fridge (this makes them easier to handle and less likely to fall apart in the pan).
3. Heat the remaining oil in a frying pan (you can use the same one used to cook the veg) and add the patties (you may need to cook these in batches). Cook for about 2–3 minutes on each side, carefully flipping over, until browned and cooked through. Serve your burgers in the toasted buns.

ELEVATE IT:
Build your burger with tomato and red onion slices, pickles, lettuce leaves, ketchup, mustard, mayo or any sauces and burger toppings of your choice.

NO WASTE – FRIDGE FORAGE:
Use up sad veg like wrinkly carrots, mushrooms and courgettes and leftover salad leaves and tomato slices in the buns.

GO VEGAN:
Use a vegan cheese instead of the Cheddar.

PICNIC LOAF

 SERVES 4-6 10 MINS V VE

Large, round crusty loaf of bread

3 heaped tbsp mayonnaise

2 heaped tbsp pesto

1 ball of mozzarella, pulled into shreds and patted dry with kitchen paper

1 packet of Parma ham, wafer-thin cooked ham or salami

3 jarred peppers, ideally a mix of yellow, red and orange, pulled into long slivers

5 jarred artichokes, drained of oil and torn into shreds

2 tbsp olive oil

Slicing this loaf to reveal layers of rainbow brights can truly turn any day into a sunshine day. I have made this super-easy by using jarred antipasti from the supermarket, but if you would prefer, feel free to chargrill or roast the peppers and artichokes (or you can use courgette) yourself. This really takes the mess out of picnics too, as it contains your usual mix of charcuterie, cheese and antipasti, all perfectly bundled up inside a bready package. Of course, you don't only have to eat this at the park . . . it's great for brunches, lunches and sunshine suppers all round.

GO VEGGIE OR VEGAN:
Leave out the ham and add extra antipasti. For vegans substitute the mayonnaise and mozzarella for vegan alternatives.

NO WASTE – FRIDGE FORAGE:
Use up sad salad like wilted rocket or basil and bruised tomatoes –just layer them up with the antipasti in the loaf!

NO WASTE – LOVE YOUR LEFTOVERS:
This is a great way to use up odd bits of charcuterie, or even shredded chicken: just pile into the layers with the other ingredients.

TIP:
To make breadcrumbs with the filling, blitz the torn dough in a processor until fine, store in an airtight container for up to a week. You can also dry the blitzed breadcrumbs in a low oven until crisp and store in an airtight container in the freezer for up to 6 months.

1. Slice the top off the loaf to create a lid. Scoop out most of the fluffy dough inside to make space for the filling (you can save this to make breadcrumbs).
2. Generously spread the inside of the hollowed-out bread and the inside of the lid with mayonnaise, then pesto.
3. Now layer up with the mozzarella, ham and vegetables, then pop the lid on and firmly press down. Wrap as tightly as possible in foil then pop into a tea towel and twist up tightly. Set aside for an hour (or store in the fridge for up to 2 days). Slice into 4–6 wedges and enjoy.

FISH (& CHIP) CAKES

SERVES 2-4 · 30 MIN

2 skinless boneless meaty white fish fillets (like cod, haddock or pollock), about 250g

Vegetable oil, for frying and drizzling

½ tin of peeled, new potatoes, drained and mashed, or 1 mug of baby new potatoes (about 175g), boiled and mashed

1 spring onion, finely snipped

1 egg

¼ mug of frozen peas, defrosted at room temperature for a few minutes

3 tbsp breadcrumbs, plus extra for coating

Lemon wedges, to serve

Ready-made tartare sauce, to serve

Fishcakes are a light little comfort in our house and these are pretty fuss-free to make in the scheme of things – no messy flour, egg, breadcrumb set up here! Freeze a few of the unfried fishcakes for quick midweek madness meals. Served with this simple and more-ish tartare sauce and maybe a splash of malt vinegar, I'm quite happy.

1. Preheat the oven to 190°C/170°C fan/Gas Mark 5. Pop the fish onto a baking tray, drizzle with a little oil and cook for 10–15 minutes until cooked through. Cool, then flake into chunks, discarding any skin and bones.
2. Mix the fish, mashed potato, spring onion, egg and peas with a little seasoning, being careful not to break the fish up too much. Mix in a few tablespoons of breadcrumbs if the mixture feels too soggy, then shape into 6–8 fishcakes.
3. Sprinkle the breadcrumbs on a tray and gently press a fishcake into the crumbs, allowing them to stick to the fishcake. Gently turn over the fish cake to crumb the other side and press more breadcrumbs into the remaining bare rim of fishcake. Repeat with the remaining fishcakes. Pop into the fridge and chill for an hour.
4. Pour just enough oil into a frying pan to cover the base and place over a medium-high heat. Fry the fishcakes (you may have to do this in batches) until golden brown and cooked through, about 3–4 minutes on each side. Serve immediately with dollops of tartare sauce.

ELEVATE IT:
Enjoy with a little fresh green salad.

NO WASTE – FRIDGE FORAGE:
This is a great way to use up leftover mashed potato.

MELTING BEEF POT

SERVES 4

3 HRS 10 MINS

1 pack of braising steak, about 500g (ideally not too lean – we want that lovely fat for flavour), cut into chunks

1 heaped tbsp plain flour

3 tbsp butter

8 small shallots or pickling onions (if you have larger ones, use fewer and cut them in half)

3 garlic cloves, crushed

2 sprigs of thyme

8 baby carrots (or 2 large carrots, quartered)

150–200g packet of button mushrooms

1 tbsp tomato ketchup

½ bottle good red wine (one you would drink!)

1 beef stock cube, crumbled

Buttery mashed potato, or warm crusty bread, to serve

Paying homage to a wonderfully famous French dish, this is a spin-off that is very easy to throw together. Not only does it taste rich and sublime but the oven does all the hard work along with the clever use of perfect-sized ingredients, like baby carrots and small shallots – the smaller the shallot or onion you can find the better; it simply means you can throw them in and they caramelise and melt down quicker, but hey, the oven is working its magic for 3 hours, so no matter what, it'll happen . . .

1. Preheat the oven to 150°C/130°C fan/Gas Mark 2.
2. Toss the steak in the flour so all the pieces are lightly coated all over.
3. Heat the butter in a large casserole over a medium-high heat until it's frothy, then add the shallots, garlic and thyme and cook for a couple minutes until the aromas hit you. Add the steak and sear until dark brown on all sides.
4. Add the carrots, mushrooms, ketchup, red wine, crumbled stock cube and a pinch of seasoning. Give everything a stir, pop the lid on then put into the oven for 3 hours until the beef is falling apart.
5. Serve with buttery mash or crusty bread.

ELEVATE IT:
Sprinkle over chopped parsley before serving.

3

LIGHTNING LUNCHES & NIFTY NIBBLES

Mostly made up of
15 minute, one-pot-ers,
these are the kind of lovely
lunchy stuff that you'll
want to be whipping up
if working (or playing)
from home.

MASALA NAAN BREAD PIZZA

 SERVES 4 15 MIN V VE

2 mugs of grated mozzarella and Cheddar cheese mix (about 250g)

4 fluffy naan bread (plain or garlic)

1–2 tbsp (depending how hot you like it) jarred jalapeño peppers, drained

½ red onion, roughly chopped

8 cherry tomatoes, halved

1 tsp ground cumin

1 tsp ground coriander

FOR THE GREEN CHUTNEY

½ bunch of mint leaves

1 bunch of coriander

Juice of 1 lemon

1 tsp ginger purée

1 tsp sugar

1 garlic clove

How incredibly cheeky is it to take supermarket naan bread and turn it into a pizza, of sorts? Very. But . . . it works really well, is ready in minutes and is extremely satisfying. The green chutney sauce really pulls it all together, so get that blitzed up in your food processor or blender and save any leftovers in the fridge or freezer to jazz up other dishes. Pre-grated mozzarella and Cheddar in bags tends to be drier than the balled version, so is perfect for this pizza.

1. Preheat the oven to 200°C/180°C fan/Gas Mark 6.
2. Sprinkle the cheese over the top the naan breads. Divide the jalapeños, red onion and tomatoes across the naan breads and finally sprinkle over the spices.
3. Pop the pizzas into the oven and bake until the cheese is bubbling and golden, about 10–15 minutes.
4. Meanwhile, make the green chutney by blitzing all the ingredients in a blender or food processor along with 4 tablespoons of water. Season to taste.
5. Serve the pizzas, generously drizzled with the green chutney.

ELEVATE IT:
Serve with dollops of mango chutney, bird's-eye chillies, rocket leaves.

NO WASTE – FRIDGE FORAGE:
Use up those sad tomatoes, while the green chutney is every floppy or wilted herb's dream!

GO VEGAN:
Substitute the cheese for a vegan alternative and make sure the naan is suitable for vegans.

ONE POTT-ANESCA

SERVES 2 · 20 MIN · VE

1 tbsp extra virgin olive oil, plus extra for drizzling

2 garlic cloves, crushed

400g tin of chopped tomatoes

1 vegetable stock cube, well crumbled

1 bunch of basil, stalks snipped, leaves whole (reserve a few to garnish)

Pinch of chilli flakes

2 x 10p-sized rounds of dried spaghetti (about 230g)

⅓ mug of black olives, pitted

2 tbsp capers, drained

Grated Parmesan cheese, to serve

This is based on a puttanesca, if you hadn't already guessed; I love a good pun almost as much as I love a one-pot pasta. This salty, umami-packed number is unbelievably simple to make (my mouth is watering as I write). You may notice that my recipe is without anchovies, but they are definitely worth adding if you like them, for some extra depth and umami – just add 4 chopped fillets with the garlic in step 1. Simple!

1. Heat the oil over a medium heat in a large, lidded saucepan, add the garlic and stir until the aromas hit you. Add the chopped tomatoes, stock cube and 1¼ tins of boiling water (use the empty tomato tin and take care as the tin will be very hot). Add the basil and chilli flakes and increase the heat to high.
2. Once the mixture begins to boil reduce the heat to medium-high and add the spaghetti, pushing it down to submerge it when you can, without breaking it.
3. Cook for 10–15 minutes, stirring regularly, until the pasta is cooked to your liking, and the sauce is thick and glossy. Stir through the olives and capers, season to taste and serve with Parmesan and the extra basil leaves.

ELEVATE IT:
Top with breadcrumbs fried in a little olive oil until crisp.

NO WASTE – FRIDGE FORAGE:
Perfect for wilty basil.

GO VEGGIE OR VEGAN:
Use a vegetarian or vegan alternative to Parmesan cheese.

ASIAN PORK LETTUCE WRAPS

 SERVES 2 **15 MIN** **VE**

1 tbsp vegetable oil or olive oil

½ packet pork or beef mince (about 250g)

Juice of 1 lime

½ tsp sugar (ideally soft dark brown, or even golden caster)

½ tbsp fish sauce

1 little gem lettuce or other small lettuce, leaves separated

FOR THE FIRECRACKER PASTE

2 spring onions, roughly snipped

2 garlic cloves, crushed

2 bird's eye chillies, stem removed

½ stalk of lemongrass, roughly snipped

These lettuce wraps are wonderful when you are after a light, fresh bite. You'll see I have stuck with fresh ingredients rather than go down the ready-made purée path, simply because the flavour here is all coming from the firecracker paste, so if you can, do try to use with the fresh chilli and lemongrass (and just let the food processor do the hard work). If I want to make this more filling, I simply add some cooked rice into the lettuce cups.

1. First make the paste: add all the ingredients to a food processor and blitz to a paste.
2. Heat the oil in a large frying pan over a medium heat and fry the paste for a couple of minutes until the aromas hit, stirring often. Add the mince and stir-fry for about 7 minutes until the meat is cooked through and browned. Then add the lime juice, sugar and fish sauce and cook for a couple more minutes, making sure you coat all the mince in the juices.
3. To serve, pile the mince into the lettuce leaves and elevate it, if you wish.

ELEVATE IT:
Customise with grated carrot, coriander leaves, mint leaves, chopped chillies, sweet chilli sauce, sriracha.

GO VEGAN:
Swap the mince for a vegan version and use vegan fish sauce (or just leave it out).

BREADY BEANS

3 tbsp extra virgin olive oil, plus extra for drizzling

3 spring onions, snipped

3 garlic cloves, crushed

400g tin of chopped tomatoes

2 x 400g tins of cannellini beans, drained

Juice of ½ lemon

1 vegetable stock cube

2 mugs of torn stale bread

1 heaped tbsp ketchup

1 tsp chilli flakes

1 bunch of basil

No offence to tinned baked beans – I love the stuff – but this simple, one-pot recipe turns them into a centrepiece with the addition of some store cupboard staples. Technically, they are no longer 'baked', but I don't think you will mind when you taste them. Stale bread works a wonder in this to pad the dish out and make those divine flavours go further. If I have some spinach that needs using up, I throw it into this dish too. So good!

1. Heat the oil over a medium heat in a large saucepan and soften the spring onion and garlic for a couple of minutes, or until the aromas hit you.
2. Add the remaining ingredients with a little seasoning and bring to the boil, then reduce the heat to low, pop the lid on and cook for about 10 minutes, keeping an eye out to make sure the bread has absorbed some liquid but isn't soggy. Season to taste, divide into bowls and enjoy.

ELEVATE IT:
Top with grated cheese, sliced cooked sausage, a fried egg.

**NO WASTE –
FRIDGE FORAGE:**
Perfect for wilty basil.

BLOODY MARY PASTA

SERVES 2 | 15 MIN | V | VE

2 x 10p-sized rounds of dried spaghetti (about 230g)

3 tbsp extra virgin olive oil

3 garlic cloves, crushed

5 tbsp tomato purée

5 tbsp vodka

½ mug of double cream

1 tbsp Worcestershire sauce (check the label to make sure it's vegetarian)

Several dashes of Tabasco

This is a winner of a midweek meal in minutes, using mostly store cupboard ingredients. Don't worry though, the alcohol cooks out, and you are left with a wonderful balance of flavours; the Worcestershire sauce and Tabasco add umami and a hit of spice. For a smidge of the time more than it takes to make a cocktail, how about you eat your Bloody Mary instead?

1. Cook the pasta according to the packet instructions.
2. Meanwhile, heat the oil over a medium heat in a large frying pan. Add the garlic and tomato purée and cook until the purée turns brown, then add the vodka and let it bubble away for a minute or so. Finally add the double cream, Worcestershire sauce and Tabasco, reduce the heat and allow to thicken.
3. Drain the pasta and transfer to the pan, along with enough of the cooking water to create a sauce that sticks to the pasta. Season to taste, being generous with the cracked black pepper. Mix well and enjoy.

ELEVATE IT:
Top with grated Parmesan cheese, basil.

GO VEGAN:
Substitute the cream for a vegan alternative.

SEARED BEEF SUMMER ROLLS & TWO DIPS

SERVES 4 · 15 MIN

2 tbsp toasted sesame oil

2 minute steaks/frying steaks

1 packet of spring roll wrappers

2 heaped tbsp peanuts, roughly crushed in a pestle and mortar

1 small packet of coleslaw mix (shredded carrot, cabbage and onion)

1 small packet of cooked rice noodles (the thinner the better)

1 chilli, finely snipped with scissors

12 mint leaves

12 sprigs of coriander

FOR THE DIPPING SAUCE (CHOOSE FROM)

Sriracha

Ready-made satay dipping sauce

Ready-made sweet chilli sauce

Crying Tiger(ish) Sauce (page 149)

We're on a roll now! Who would have thought replicating(ish) an Asian classic could be so easy? Supermarket coleslaw mix is perfect for the crunch needed in a summer roll, as are ready-to-go dipping sauces! (Now is not the time to be making sweet chilli sauce from scratch, people.) I have also gone a bit rogue with the rolling here, no fiddly full enclosing, just think mini burrito and you are there. Any leftover ingredients can be mixed together for a divine fresh noodle salad for the next day.

1. Heat the toasted sesame oil in a frying pan over a high heat. Season both sides of the steaks and fry for a minute on each side, then let rest on a plate, tented with foil. When cool enough to handle, use scissors to snip into thin finger-width strips.
2. Working one at a time, pop the rice paper wrappers in a bowl of warm water for about 10 seconds until they soften, then drain on a tea towel.
3. Pop a small mix of all the ingredients in the middle of the wrapper, roll the bottom up a little then roll the sides tightly together, to make an almost mini burrito.
4. Repeat with the remaining wrappers and ingredients, then serve with your choice of dipping sauce.

SRIRACHA HONEY CHEESE TOASTIE

SERVES 1 | 15 MIN | V

2 thick slices of good-quality bread (white is great for this)

Butter, for spreading and frying

1 tsp Dijon mustard, for spreading

½ tbsp runny honey mixed with 1 tbsp sriracha

1 mug (not packed) of a mix of grated Cheddar and ready-grated mozzarella or Gruyère cheese

Cheese toasties have always been a source of quick comfort, but how taking it to another level with a hint of spice and sweetness? If you don't have mozzarella or Gruyère, don't worry, just stick with Cheddar, but do try to get your hands on some for the next time. You can often find ready-grated bags pretty cheaply in supermarkets; they are perfect to throw into a toastie along with our Cheddar stalwart and you'll get that lovely cheesy pull that we all want from a toasted cheese sandwich!

1. Generously butter both sides of each slice of bread, followed by a scant spread of the mustard. Generously drizzle the honey sriracha on one side of each slice. Scatter the cheese evenly over each slice.

2. Pop a tablespoon of butter into a large frying pan over a medium heat. Once it is frothy, carefully pop the cheese scattered slices of bread, cheese-side up, into the pan. Cover the pan with a lid and cook until the cheese is beginning to become gooey and melted, about 5 minutes.

3. Remove the lid, then carefully sandwich the 2 slices together and pop a small heavy pan on top of the toastie, or press down with a spatula, and continue to cook until the sandwich is golden all over, carefully flipping over a few times, about 2–5 minutes (if the bread looks like it is burning, reduce the heat). Eat immediately.

ELEVATE IT:
Serve with chutney or pickles.

SA(D)LAD
PESTO

SERVES 8 · 10 MIN · VE

1 small bag of any mix of dark salad leaves (about 60–80g)
1 small packet of basil (about 20g)
2 garlic cloves, crushed
10 heaped tbsp pine nuts (about 120g), toasted
1 packed mug of grated Parmesan cheese (about 100g)
1 mug extra virgin olive oil
Juice of 1 lemon

Yes, we all love making pesto to use up herbs, but here is a lovely twist that uses up sad leafy salad. I find dark salad leaves like watercress, rocket, lambs lettuce and spinach work best. You can switch the herbs and nuts too if you like. Don't be restricted to pasta when it comes to this pesto; use it to elevate salads, roasted veg, cooked meats and other leftovers.

1. Pulse all the ingredients in a food processor, adding half the oil initially, and trickling in the rest (you may not want to use all, or you may want more!) until the desired consistency is reached; I like a little texture to mine.
2. Season well and store in an airtight container, topping up with a little oil to preserve the colour, in the fridge for up to 3 days, or in the freezer.

GO VEGGIE OR VEGAN:
Substitute the Parmesan for a veggie or vegan alternative.

CRISPY HALLOUMI & HOT HONEY

SERVES 4 · 15 MIN · V

1 tsp rose harissa paste

4 tbsp runny honey

Vegetable oil, for frying

8 heaped tbsp plain flour

2 tsp paprika

2 tsp garlic granules

2 x 250g blocks of halloumi, (straight from the packet as the liquid on the cheese helps the flour to stick), cut into chips

This went down a storm during recipe-testing. It's an incredibly easy, one-dunk way to make a crispy-outside-gooey-inside cheese. The saltiness of the halloumi bathed in the harissa honey balances so beautifully. I often make this into a meal with a flatbread and a light rocket salad.

1. Whisk together the harissa paste and the honey until well combined.
2. Pour enough vegetable oil into a deep-sided frying pan to completely cover the base and come up to a depth of about 1cm. Place over a medium-high heat until hot.
3. Mix the flour, paprika and garlic granules with a generous pinch of sea salt flakes. Dunk the halloumi into the flour, shake off any excess and carefully place in the hot oil, frying for a couple minutes on all sides, until golden. Serve immediately, drizzled with the hot harissa honey.

CHEATSY CHEESE & CHORIZO ROUGH SCONES

MAKES 5-6 · 30 MIN · V

1 packed mug of self-raising flour (250g), plus extra for dusting

1 tsp paprika (smoked or sweet)

1 chorizo ring, skinned and crumbled

1 mug of grated Cheddar cheese (or Manchego for an extra special touch)

2 x 120g pots of natural yoghurt

2 tbsp milk, to glaze

There's nothing like a warm scone, thickly spread with salty butter and a slab of cheese. These are simple to make and a great way to get the kids involved in the kitchen. Don't worry about them looking perfect, they are called rough for a reason and you won't have to worry about rerolling any scraps as you would when using a round cutter!

1. Preheat the oven to 200°C/180°C/Gas Mark 6 and put a baking sheet inside to heat up.
2. Tip the flour, paprika and chorizo into a bowl with the grated cheese, reserving a little cheese for the tops of the scones. Add a pinch of salt and mix well, then mix in the yoghurt until the dough just comes together. Knead a few times until smooth.
3. On a floured surface, press the dough out to the thickness of about 1cm, then cut into 6 equal sized square scones. Sprinkle over the reserved cheese.
4. Pop onto the heated baking sheet and then into the oven for 20 minutes, or until risen and cooked through.

ELEVATE IT:
Serve warm with cheese, eggs, butter.

GO VEGGIE:
Just leave out the chorizo or substitute with a vegetarian version.

HANSEL & GRETEL SPAGHETTI

SERVES 4 · 15 MIN · VE

4 x 10p-sized rounds of dried uncooked spaghetti (about 460g)

2 tbsp olive oil

2 large garlic cloves, crushed

Zest and juice of 1 lemon

¾ mug of breadcrumbs

4 tbsp extra virgin olive oil

1 tsp chilli flakes

Grated Parmesan cheese, to serve

What's not to love about this double-carb pasta? Can you honestly tell me you don't already have these ingredients in your kitchen? It's the perfect low-cost midweek meal to throw together in minutes. I often gravitate to this when I see a stale loaf of bread on the counter that needs using up.

1. Cook the spaghetti according to the packet instructions.
2. Meanwhile, heat the olive oil in a large frying pan over a medium heat. Add the garlic, lemon zest and breadcrumbs and cook until golden and crisp, then remove from the pan so the breadcrumbs don't continue to cook.
3. Add the cooked spaghetti to the same pan, along with the lemon juice, extra virgin olive oil, chilli flakes and ½ mug of the spaghetti cooking water. Toss well, then divide between dishes and top with the crispy breadcrumbs and grated Parmesan. Season with black pepper and serve.

ELEVATE IT:
Add a handful of basil or parsley leaves, tossed through with the cooked spaghetti, so they wilt.

GO VEGGIE OR VEGAN:
Just omit the Parmesan or use a vegan alternative.

LAZY LAKSA

 SERVES 4 15 MIN VE

2 tbsp sesame oil (or use olive or veg oil)

2–3 heaped tbsp Thai red curry paste (depending on how spicy you want it)

2 garlic cloves, crushed

2 spring onions, finely snipped

1 heaped tbsp peanut butter

2 mugs of freezer Chicken Strippers (see page 188), or 4 skinless chicken thigh fillets, snipped into thin slivers (or 1 mug of king prawns or shredded leftover cooked chicken)

400ml tin of coconut milk

1 vegetable stock cube, crumbled

Juice of 2 limes

2 jarred peppers, torn into slivers

4 nests of egg noodles

Slurpy, saucy, spicy noodles are my weak spot and this 15-minute belter really hits it hard. Quite often I just leave out the chicken (but it's a great way to use those freezer Chicken Strippers!) and enjoy the noodles as they are, boiling off more of the liquid to make a richer, slurpier noodle, so go with what you have and how you feel.

1. Heat the oil in a large saucepan over a medium heat. Add the Thai red curry paste, garlic, spring onions and peanut butter and fry for a couple of minutes. Add the chicken (or prawns) and fry for another couple of minutes.
2. Add the coconut milk and 4 tins of just-boiled water, using the empty coconut milk tin (careful, it will be hot), the crumbled stock cube, the lime juice and the peppers. Bring to the boil, then reduce to the lowest simmer.
3. Add the noodles, cover and cook for another 5 minutes until the noodles have softened and the chicken or prawns are cooked through. Enjoy.

ELEVATE IT:
Serve with lime wedges, fresh coriander, snipped red chillies.

NO WASTE – LOVE YOUR LEFTOVERS:
Perfect for leftover cooked chicken – just shred it and throw it in for the last 5 minutes until piping hot through.

GO VEGGIE OR VEGAN:
Just leave out the chicken, or swap it for chunks of sweet potato, baby corn, sweetcorn, mushrooms or aubergine. To make it vegan, substitute the egg noodles for a vegan alternative.

CORONATION CHICKEN RICE SALAD

 SERVES **4**

 15 MIN

1 tbsp vegetable oil

2 heaped tsp mild curry powder

5 heaped tbsp mayonnaise

2 heaped tbsp crème fraîche

2 tbsp mango chutney

3 heaped tbsp raisins

3 heaped tbsp toasted flaked almonds, plus extra to serve

4 skinless chicken fillets, roasted or poached, then cooled and shredded (or about 1–2 mugs of cold leftover chicken, shredded)

1½ mugs of cooked rice, or 1 packet of microwave rice, cooled

2 little gem lettuces, leaves separated into 'cups' (optional)

I have a thing for coronation chicken. This version is simple and works perfectly on cold leftover chicken that has been shredded, but of course you can cook (as I often do) the chicken from scratch, as below. The same goes for the rice too. Serving this in lettuce cups is a clever way to make it look a little sophisticated, if that's what you are after!

1. In a small frying pan, heat the oil over a medium heat and fry the curry powder, stirring continuously until the aromas are released and a paste has formed. Set aside to cool.
2. Empty the paste into a bowl and mix in the mayonnaise, crème fraiche, mango chutney, raisins and almonds. Add the shredded chicken and a pinch of seasoning and stir until well combined. Finally fold through the rice.
3. Divide among the lettuce cups, if you wish, and sprinkle over the extra flaked almonds.

ELEVATE IT:
Add finely chopped coriander leaves.

NO WASTE – FRIDGE FORAGE:
Great for using up leftover chicken and rice.

BANG BANG RAINBOW SALAD

SERVES 2 · 15 MIN · VE

2 skinless chicken fillets, roasted or poached, then cooled and shredded (or about 1-2 mugs of shredded cold leftover chicken or pork)

1 cucumber, seeds scooped out with a spoon and ribboned using a vegetable peeler

1 packet of ready-made coleslaw mix

2 spring onions, finely snipped

½ bunch of coriander, leaves picked

½ small tin of pineapple chunks (about 100g)

1 large red chilli, finely snipped

FOR THE BANG BANG SAUCE

5 heaped tbsp peanut butter (smooth or chunky)

1 tbsp toasted sesame oil

1 tbsp soy sauce

1 tbsp honey

1 garlic clove, crushed

1 tsp ginger paste

Juice of ½ lime, to taste

Lime wedges, to serve

This is a real a keeper of a recipe, one to have ready to go, especially if you can get your coleslaw ingredients ready shredded from the supermarket, and regardless of whether you have leftover meats or not. It is fresh and light and perfect for meals in moments.

1. Mix together the chicken or pork, cucumber, coleslaw mix, spring onions, coriander, pineapple and chilli in a large bowl.
2. Stir together the peanut butter, sesame oil, soy sauce, honey, garlic and ginger until smooth, adding lime juice to taste. Drizzle over the salad and toss then enjoy immediately, with lemon wedges for squeezing over.

ELEVATE IT:
Sprinkle over toasted sesame seeds before serving.

NO WASTE – LOVE YOUR LEFTOVERS:
Great to use up leftover chicken or pork.

GO VEGGIE OR VEGAN:
Swap the chicken or pork for chickpeas or roasted vegetables that need using up. To make it vegan, swap the honey for maple syrup or agave nectar.

HASTY (& TASTY) HUMMUS

400g tin of chickpeas, drained*

2 tbsp tahini

2 garlic cloves, peeled

½ mug of water

Juice of 1 lemon, to taste

4 tbsp olive oil, plus extra for drizzling

Hummus is often relegated to the role of sidekick, but here I'm giving it the spotlight with four different tag-along twists – or rather toppings – making it a meal in itself. Save the chickpea water (aquafaba) to make Black Forest Mousse (see page 172).

1. Blitz all the ingredients, except the lemon juice and the olive oil, until the consistency is smooth. Add the remaining ingredients, mix and season to taste.

STICKY TOMATO TOPPING

3 tbsp olive oil, for frying

1 garlic clove, crushed

1 tsp dried oregano

1 tbsp balsamic vinegar

2 mugs or 1 small packet of cherry or vine tomatoes (about 300g)

Flatbread or pitta, or cooked grains, to serve

1. Heat the olive oil in a large frying pan over a medium heat. Add the garlic and oregano, and stir until the aromas hit you, then add the balsamic vinegar. Allow it to bubble a little then add the tomatoes a good whack of sea salt and stir. Pop the lid on and cook, stirring now and again, until the tomatoes are wilted and sticky, about 15 minutes. Serve on top of your hummus, with all the toppings you wish.

CHORIZO, SPINACH & PEPPER TOPPING

2 x 60g packets of diced chorizo, or ½ cured chorizo ring, snipped into 1-cm discs

2 jarred roasted red peppers, snipped into thin slivers

2 handfuls of spinach

Flatbread or pitta, or cooked grains, to serve

1. Place a frying pan over a medium-high heat. Add the chorizo and peppers and cook until the chorizo crisps up, about 5 minutes, stirring often and adding the spinach at the end to wilt. Mix well and serve on top of your hummus, along with all the toppings you wish and flatbread or pitta for dipping.

CREAMY HARISSA FETA & MINTY PEA TOPPING

 SERVES 2 5 MIN V VE

1 packet of feta

1 heaped tbsp plain Greek yoghurt

1 garlic clove

2 tbsp rose harissa paste

Generous splash of olive oil

½ mug of frozen peas, left in just-boiled water until room temperature, then drained

5 mint leaves, torn

Flatbread or pitta, or cooked grains, to serve

1. In a blender, or food processor, blitz the feta, yoghurt, garlic, harissa paste and olive oil, along with enough water to make it creamy, then season to taste. Serve on top of your hummus, along with the peas, mint leaves and any other toppings you wish and flatbread or pitta for dipping.

ELEVATE IT:
Add drizzles of extra virgin olive oil, toasted pine nuts.

GO VEGAN:
Substitute the feta and Greek yoghurt for a vegan alternative.

CRISPY LAMB TOPPING

 SERVES 2 20 MIN

1 tbsp olive oil

½ pack lamb mince (about 200g)

1 tsp ground cumin

1 tsp ground allspice

½ mug of raisins

2 spring onions, snipped

2 tbsp toasted pine nuts

10 mint leaves, torn or snipped with scissors

¼ bunch of parsley, snipped

Flatbread or pitta, or cooked grains, to serve

1. Heat the olive oil in a large frying pan over a high heat. Add the lamb mince and fry, stirring often and breaking it up with a wooden spoon, for about 5 minutes until browned all over. Add the spices, raisins and spring onions along with a pinch of seasoning and continue to stir-fry for another 5 minutes or so, reducing the heat to medium-high and stirring very often, until the lamb is crispy and cooked. Serve on top of your hummus, scattered with the pine nuts, mint and parsley leaves and flatbread or pitta for dipping.

Sticky Tomato
Topping

Creamy Harissa
Feta & Minty
Pea Topping

Crispy Lamb Topping

Chorizo, Spinach & Pepper Topping

MEAL MATHEMATICS

I've done the hard recipe equations so you can walk away with A* quicksie meals tailored to the flavours you like and the ingredients you want to use (or need to use up!). So chop and change each time round for a different result. Quite possibly my favourite (and most used) chapter.

WRAPPER'S DELIGHT

SERVES 2 · 15 MIN · VE

Not only am I thrilled about the recipe title here (chuckling away to myself), but this is one of my favourite ways to create a quick meal, using up odds and ends and leftovers but without any compromise on flavour or texture. Make it your own depending on what you have lying around and what tickles your fancy, so add and remove ingredients from each section as you see fit. You can also set up a great DIY station with all the ingredients ready to go so if you are feeding more than two, they can all dive in and help themselves.

FOR THE BASE

2 large tortilla wraps

2 heaped tbsp mayonnaise

FOR THE FILLING (CHOOSE FROM)

- ✗ 4 chicken goujons
- ✗ 4 fish goujons or fingers
- ✗ 1 block of halloumi in thick slices
- ✗ Leftover cooked meat
- ✗ Leftover cooked roasted veg (e.g. sweet potatoes, Sunday Roast veg, aubergine, peppers, red onions)

FOR FLAVOUR

- ✗ 1 tbsp chipotle paste
- ✗ 1 tbsp jerk paste
- ✗ 1 tbsp rose harissa paste
- ✗ 1 tbsp pesto

FOR TEXTURE (CHOOSE AS MANY AS YOU LIKE)

- ✗ 2 large lettuce leaves, rolled and snipped into thin shreds
- ✗ 2 large cabbage leaves, rolled and snipped into thin shreds
- ✗ 1 tomato, sliced
- ✗ Jarred jalapeños, to taste
- ✗ ½–1 avocado, sliced
- ✗ 1–2 tbsp sweetcorn
- ✗ 1–2 jarred peppers
- ✗ 1–2 tbsp cooked peas

GO VEGGIE OR VEGAN:
Simply choose veggie or vegan elements in your wrap!

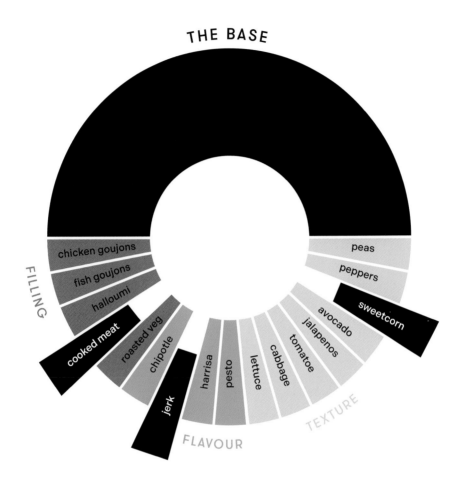

THE BASE

FILLING
- chicken goujons
- fish goujons
- halloumi
- cooked meat
- roasted veg

FLAVOUR
- chipotle
- jerk
- harrisa
- pesto

TEXTURE
- lettuce
- cabbage
- tomatoe
- jalapenos
- avocado
- sweetcorn
- peppers
- peas

1. Decide on your filling and cook, if necessary, according to the packet instructions (if using leftovers you can enjoy the wrap cold). For halloumi, pop the slices under a hot grill for a few minutes until golden, flipping over halfway through.

2. In the meantime, heat the tortilla wraps in a large dry frying pan over a low heat.

3. Divide the mayo and your chosen paste between the wraps, swirling and spreading them across the surface. Add texture by adding as many additional ingredients as you like, then wrap and enjoy.

BUILD ME UP BUTTERCUP BOARD

SERVES 4-6 · 10 MINS · V

I've been hit by the TikTok stick (once again) … Based on Justine Doiron's beautiful Butter Board, I've whipped up the perfect serve for you, to swipe and load your hunks of warm bread: whether for a TV snack, for the family as a lazy lunch, or a stunning snack board for dinner parties. Go on … *Spread Your Things.*

FOR THE BASE (CHOOSE FROM)

- ✕ **Butter**
- ✕ **Boursin**
- ✕ **Gorgonzola/Dolcelatte**
- ✕ **Cream cheese**

(about 150-250g, at room temperature, so easily spreadable)

FOR FLAVOUR (CHOOSE FROM)

- ✕ 1 heaped tbsp runny honey mixed with 1 tsp (rose) harissa paste
- ✕ 1 heaped tsp chipotle paste, loosened to a drizzling consistency with olive oil
- ✕ 1 heaped tbsp pesto, loosened to a drizzling consistency with olive oil
- ✕ 1 heaped tbsp caramelised onion, loosened to a drizzling consistency with olive oil
- ✕ ½ tbsp Marmite, loosened to a drizzling consistency with olive oil

FOR TEXTURE (CHOOSE FROM)

(about 1-2 heaped tbsp)
- ✕ Chorizo Lemon Crumb (see page 153)
- ✕ Fried Herby Capers (see page 153)
- ✕ Mixed roasted seeds or nuts
- ✕ Dukkah

TOPPERS (CHOOSE AS MANY AS YOU LIKE)

- ✕ Rocket leaves
- ✕ 2 tbsp sundried or sun-blushed tomatoes, snipped or torn into smaller slivers
- ✕ 1 small packet of cured ham (salami, chorizo, prosciutto) pulled into smaller strands
- ✕ Strands of parsley
- ✕ Basil leaves
- ✕ Zest of ½ lemon or lime
- ✕ Edible flowers
- ✕ Chilli flakes
- ✕ Hunks or thick slices of bread of your choice, to serve

1. Grab a large serving board or platter and artistically spread the softened base across the board or platter along with a sprinkling of sea salt flakes (if you've used salted butter, leave out this step).
2. Drizzle and sprinkle over your choice of flavour, texture and toppers, being careful to evenly spread the ingredients. Depending on the size of your board and the amount of base you have, use as little or as much of the flavour, texture and toppers to give a generous-looking board, without it being too crowded.

FOCACCIAZZA

SERVES 4-6 · 20 MIN · VE

Who doesn't love a fluffy deep-pan pizza? Especially when all you have to do is choose and pile on your favourite toppings. This is a perfectly cheatsy recipe that makes the most of supermarket focaccia: great to involve the kids, leaves minimal washing-up and is so delicious. Try to buy the largest focaccia you can find and experiment with your own favourite toppings.

2 x 400g ready-made focaccias (or as large as you can find)
Extra virgin olive oil, for drizzling
Green salad, to serve

FOR FLAVOUR
4 heaped tbsp tomato purée
1 heaped tsp oregano
½ tsp garlic granules

OR

4 heaped tbsp pesto

OR

2–3 heaped tbsp rose harissa paste

OR

2–3 heaped tbsp chipotle paste

CHEESE (CHOOSE FROM)

- ✕ 1 mug of ready-grated mozzarella
- ✕ ½ block of feta, crumbled
- ✕ 1 small pack (about 100g) goat's cheese, crumbled or spread
- ✕ 1 mug of grated Cheddar cheese

TOPPINGS (CHOOSE AS MANY AS YOU LIKE)

- ✕ 1 small packet of sliced chorizo/salami/Parma ham/cooked ham
- ✕ 1 small jar of sliced black olives
- ✕ 1 heaped tbsp caramelised onion
- ✕ ½ mug of shredded cooked chicken
- ✕ 1–2 jarred peppers, pulled into long shreds
- ✕ 1 chilli, snipped

FOR CRUNCH (CHOOSE FROM)

- ✕ 2 tbsp Chorizo Lemon Crumb (see page 153)
- ✕ 2 tbsp Fried Herby Capers (see page 153)
- ✕ 2 tbsp mixed seeds
- ✕ 2 tbsp toasted pine nuts

GO VEGGIE OR VEGAN:
Simply choose veggie or vegan elements on your pizza!

1. Preheat the oven to 220°C/200°C fan/ Gas Mark 7.
2. Pop the focaccia onto a large baking tray and spread (or sprinkle) with your chosen flavour. Add the cheese and toppings of your choice, drizzle over a little extra virgin olive oil, then pop into the oven for about 10–15 minutes until the cheese is bubbling.
3. Add your choice of crunch, then slice up and serve immediately.

THE BASE

FLAVOUR

purée, oregano, garlic
pesto
harissa
chipotle

CHEESE

mozzarella
feta
goats cheese
cheddar
chorizo/salami/ham
black olives

TOPPINGS

caramelised onion
shredded chicken
jarred peppers
chilli
lemon crumb
capers

CRUNCH

toasted pine nuts
mixed seeds

FRIED RICE MATHEMATICS

SERVES 2 · 10 MIN · VE

My go-to for leftover rice, this is more of an equation than a recipe, but it's perfect for a quick meal that uses up odds and ends and the like. Make it your own depending on what you have in the fridge and what you are in the mood for, so go forth and multi-fry!

FOR THE BASE

2 tbsp sesame oil (or use olive or vegetable oil)
2 spring onions, snipped
2 mugs of cooked rice (cold leftover rice is ideal, or use 1–2 pouches of microwave rice)

FOR THE FILLING (CHOOSE FROM)

✕ Leftover cooked meats (chicken, beef, pork or lamb), shredded or minced
✕ Leftover cooked roasted veg (e.g. sweet potatoes, Sunday Roast veg, aubergine, peppers, red onions)
✕ Leftover charcuterie (e.g. chorizo, ham, salami slices)

FOR TEXTURE (CHOOSE AS MANY AS YOU LIKE)

✕ ½ mug of frozen peas
✕ ½ mug of frozen sweetcorn or frozen mixed veg
✕ Sesame seeds
✕ Torn mushrooms
✕ Grated carrot
✕ Cabbage leaves, rolled and snipped into shreds

FOR FLAVOUR

1 tbsp maple syrup
1 egg, beaten
Soy sauce, to taste
Chilli oil, to taste

1. Heat the oil in a large frying pan or wok over a medium-high heat. Soften the spring onions for a couple minutes then add any raw veg, stirring continuously for a couple minutes.
2. Add the rice, your choice of filling and any texture additions and cook until everything is piping hot through, stirring often.
3. Add the maple syrup and stir through, then add the beaten egg, stirring continuously until the egg has cooked. Season to taste with salt and pepper, adding soy sauce and chilli oil to taste.

THE BASE

FILLING
- leftover meat
- leftover veg
- leftover charcutie
- frozen peas

TEXTURE
- frozen veg
- sesame seeds
- torn mushrooms
- grated carrot
- cabbage leaves

FLAVOUR
- maple syrup
- egg
- soy sauce
- chilli

GO VEGGIE OR VEGAN:
Simply choose veggie or vegan elements with your rice.

SOLVE ALL CURRY SAUCE

SERVES 8 | 20 MIN | VE

This is an essential store cupboard recipe. With this in hand, no matter what you have lying around you'll be able to whip up a tasty meal, whether you are using up sad ingredients or leftovers or just fancy a simple and quick curry!

1 tbsp vegetable oil

2 onions, peeled and blitzed in a food processor until roughly chopped

3 large garlic cloves, crushed

1 heaped tbsp ginger purée

3 heaped tbsp curry powder

2 tbsp ground cumin

1–2 tsp chilli powder (depending on how hot you want it)

2 x 400g tins of coconut milk

400g tin of chopped tomatoes

1. Heat the oil in a large saucepan over a medium heat. Add the onions, garlic and ginger and cook, stirring often, until caramelised and softened, about 10 minutes. Add the spices and cook until the aromas fill the air, about 20 seconds, stirring continuously.
2. Add the coconut milk, chopped tomatoes and a little seasoning. Bring to the boil, then reduce to a simmer and season to taste. If you just want to keep the curry sauce ready to go, store in an airtight container in the fridge for up to 3 days, or freeze for up to 6 months.
3. At this stage you can add your protein and veg and continue to cook until the sauce is rich and the added ingredients are cooked through.

ELEVATE IT:
Elevates: Sad veg like spinach, sweet potato, squash, aubergine and cauliflower. Odds and ends like that half tin of chickpeas, raw chicken or lamb, fish or shellfish. Leftovers, like cooked chicken and lamb. Just make sure any raw ingredients are cooked through and leftovers are piping hot through before serving.

MEAL MATHEMATICS

PEANUT & GINGER SAUCE

This is a super-speedy sauce that you can use to elevate noodle-based dishes, rice-based dishes, stir-fries, raw crunchy veg salads, roasted veg, grilled meat skewers like chicken, beef and pork, prawns – this list is endless!

4 tbsp sesame oil

10 tbsp peanut butter

4 tsp soy sauce

4 tsp honey

2 tsp ginger purée

1 large garlic clove, crushed

1. Whisk together all the ingredients until smooth, using hot water to loosen to a sauce-like consistency. Season to taste.

2. Store in an airtight container in the fridge for up to 5 days, or freeze in ice-cube trays.

GO VEGAN:
Swap the honey for agave syrup or maple syrup.

PIMPED PACKET NOODLE RAMEN

SERVES 2 · 10 MIN · VE

There is something so wonderfully comforting about a bowl of ramen noodles, whatever the season. This version uses packet ramen – don't turn your nose up at it; I assure you that with the added flavours, veg and protein, it becomes something spectacular, and amazingly easy to accomplish. This is one to elevate to your heart's content – you really can't go too OTT with this. Have it slurpy or dry as you like.

FOR THE BASE

2 tbsp toasted sesame oil
1 spring onion (white bulb discarded), snipped
1 tsp garlic purée
2 mugs of boiling water
2 packets of ramen noodles (or any other instant noodles)

OR

300g ready-cooked noodles and
1 chicken stock cube, crumbled

OR

300g ready-cooked noodles and
2 sachets of miso soup mix

FOR THE PROTEIN (CHOOSE FROM)

✕ 1 mug of frozen, fresh (raw) or cooked chicken strips
✕ 1 mug of frozen, fresh (raw) or cooked seafood
✕ 1 mug of frozen or fresh gyoza dumplings
✕ ½ block of firm tofu, broken into smaller pieces

FOR THE VEG

250g packet of pak choi, leaves separated
½ mug of frozen vegetables

TOPPERS (CHOOSE AS MANY AS YOU LIKE)

✕ Soft-boiled egg halves
✕ Drizzles of chilli oil
✕ 1 tbsp sesame seeds
✕ Fresh coriander sprigs
✕ Fresh chillies
✕ Kimchi
✕ Drizzles of sriracha

**GO VEGAN
OR VEGAN:**
Simply choose veggie
or vegan elements
with your noodles!

1. Heat the oil in a small saucepan over a medium heat and cook the spring onion and garlic purée for a couple minutes, stirring often until aromatic.

2. Add the boiling water, along with the dried noodles and their flavour sachets, or the cooked noodles with the crumbled stock cube or the miso soup sachets. Stir together and cook for a minute or two until the liquid is mostly absorbed.

3. Add your chosen protein and the veg and cook until the protein is just cooked through, about 5 minutes or so. If you are using fresh chicken or seafood it will take less time. If using tofu, add in the last few minutes so it doesn't disintegrate.

4. Serve into bowls and go crazy with the toppers.

NO-STIR RISOTTO

SERVES 4 · 20 MIN · V

No stir, you say? I say yes: not only is this baked version full of fresh flavours but you won't be stirring (or slaving!) over a hot stove, leaving the hard work to the oven. Such a great recipe to use up sad veg. You can mix and match the flavours and finishes as you wish – mascarpone works really beautifully with the tomato and lemon combo as well as with beetroot.

FOR THE BASE

2 tbsp butter
4 spring onions, finely snipped
2 garlic cloves, crushed
2 mugs of risotto rice (about 400g)
2 stock cubes dissolved in 2½ mugs (750ml) boiling water and kept warm in a saucepan
¾ mug of grated Parmesan cheese

FINISHERS

✗ Zest of 1 lemon
✗ 2 heaped tbsp mascarpone
✗ 1 tsp chilli flakes

TOPPERS

✗ Extra lemon zest
✗ Toasted pine nuts
✗ Your choice of Rubble Trouble (see page 152)
✗ Drizzle of extra virgin olive oil
✗ Basil leaves
✗ Handful of breadcrumbs, shallow-fried in olive oil until crisp

FOR FLAVOUR

✗ 1 small bag (about 300g) of cherry or baby tomatoes
Juice of ½ lemon

OR

✗ 1 bag of ready-cut squash (about 350–500g)
¼ bunch of sage leaves

OR

✗ 1 mug of frozen peas, left to defrost at room temperature
1 packet of ham, torn into shreds

OR

✗ 3 heaped tbsp dried mushrooms, covered with boiling water to rehydrate (or use a heaped mug of fresh mushrooms, torn)
¼ packet of parsley

OR

✗ 1 small packet of steamed beetroot, grated

NO WASTE – LOVE YOUR LEFTOVERS:
Turn any leftover risotto into arancini by rolling into small balls, dunking in breadcrumbs and frying until golden on all sides.

GO VEGGIE:
Choose veggie elements for your risotto and omit the Parmesan.

1. Preheat the oven to 200°C/180°C fan/ Gas Mark 6.
2. Melt the butter in a large ovenproof casserole dish or saucepan over a medium heat. Add the spring onions and garlic and cook for about 2 minutes. Add the rice and stir to coat all the grains.
3. Add your chosen flavour, the stock and a pinch of seasoning and give everything a stir, then pop the lid on and bake in the oven for about 15–20 minutes until just cooked, (if adding the peas, do so in the last 5 minutes of cooking).
4. Stir through most of the Parmesan plus your choice of finisher. Serve immediately with the remaining Parmesan and any toppers.

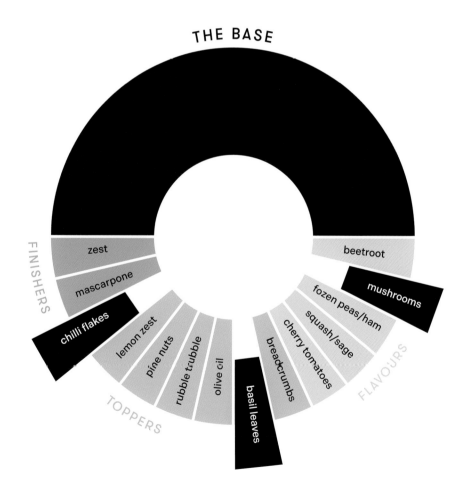

THE BASE

FINISHERS
zest
mascarpone
chilli flakes

TOPPERS
lemon zest
pine nuts
rubble trubble
olive oil
basil leaves

FLAVOURS
beetroot
mushrooms
fozen peas/ham
squash/sage
cherry tomatoes
breadcrumbs

NO-CHOP CHOPPED SALAD

SERVES 4 · 15 MIN · V

A salad for me has to be of epic meal proportions and leave me full and satisfied. This one ticks all the beautiful boxes, plus some more because the star of the show here is actually a kitchen tool – the pizza cutter. No faffing about with slicing a ton of salad and veg; a bowl and the pizza cutter does it all. Using bags of ready-prepared ingredients also cuts the job down immensely, so don't feel guilty about getting all the shortcuts you want. If you do go down this route, look for bags that have loads of colourful veg in them too – like sweetcorn, pepper, carrot. It's all about tasting the rainbow!

FOR THE SALAD

✕ 1 head of lettuce or large bag of mixed leaves
½ cucumber
2 spring onions
2 jarred peppers
1 mug of cherry tomatoes
1 large carrot, grated
½ mug of sweetcorn, left to defrost at room temperature if frozen

OR

✕ use 1 large (or 2 small) packets of ready-prepared mixed salad (leaves, salad and veg)

FOR THE PROTEIN
(CHOOSE FROM, OR COMBINE TOGETHER)

✕ 1 small packet of sliced cooked chicken, crumbled into smaller pieces

OR

✕ 1 mug of cooked prawns (defrosted safely if using from frozen)

✕ 1 small packet of cooked bacon, crumbled into smaller pieces

OR

✕ 1 small packet of sliced cooked ham or cured ham (salami, chorizo, prosciutto), pulled into smaller pieces

✕ ½–1 mug of crumbled or grated cheese (blue cheese, feta, Cheddar)

✕ 2–4 hard-boiled eggs, peeled

FOR A CAESAR-STYLE DRESSING

½ mug of mayonnaise
1 garlic clove crushed
1 tbsp extra virgin olive oil
2 heaped tbsp grated Parmesan cheese
1 heaped tsp Dijon mustard
Juice of ½ lemon

FOR A HONEY MUSTARD DRESSING

4 tbsp Dijon mustard
4 tbsp runny honey
1 garlic clove crushed
4 tbsp olive oil
Juice of ½ lemon

MEAL MATHEMATICS

FOR CRUNCH (CHOOSE FROM)

✕ 1 mug of Rubble Trouble (see page 152)
✕ 1 small packet of croutons
✕ 2 tbsp mixed seed and nuts

1. Pop all your salad ingredients (or supermarket bags of mixed salad), except for the carrot and sweetcorn, into a large bowl. Take your pizza cutter and roll back and forth over your salad for a few minutes until the ingredients are all nicely chopped. Then add the carrot and sweetcorn.
2. Add your chosen protein. If adding hard-boiled egg, run your pizza cutter over it lightly to chop into smaller pieces (but without making it disintegrate completely).
3. Pop all the ingredients for your chosen dressing into a mug and whisk with a fork, then season to taste.
4. Add the dressing to the bowl and toss through the salad and protein. Divide into bowls to serve and top with your chosen crunch!

GO VEGGIE:
Simply choose veggie
elements for your
salad!

MAKE A PIE OF IT

SERVES 4 · 45 MIN · VE

Puff pastry should be part of the furniture in your freezer. It is literally a canvas on which you can throw a range of toppings and leftovers to create a delicious meal with hardly any effort. Mix and match your flavours, toppings and textures, depending on what you have lying around or what you fancy. I love the freeform galette-style of this tart; it basically means you don't need to worry about how the tart looks as this is 'rustic' food at its best!

FOR THE BASE

1 sheet of ready-rolled puff pastry
1 beaten egg, to glaze
Olive oil, for drizzling

FOR FLAVOUR (CHOOSE FROM)

- ✕ 1 heaped tbsp pesto
- ✕ 1 heaped tbsp caramelised onion
- ✕ ½–1 tbsp harissa paste
  (depending on how spicy you like it)
- ✕ 1 heaped tbsp soft cheese
  (goat's cheese works well)

FOR THE TOPPINGS (CHOOSE FROM)

- ✕ 1 small packet (about 200g) of
  sundried or sun-blushed tomatoes
- ✕ 2 jarred peppers, snipped into slivers
- ✕ ½ mug of grated cheese
- ✕ 1 packet of asparagus tips, cooked
- ✕ ½ mug of black olives
- ✕ Ready-sliced cured chorizo, serrano
  or cooked ham or cooked chicken
- ✕ ½ block of feta, crumbled
- ✕ ⅓ mug of frozen peas, left to
  defrost at room temperature for 5 minutes
- ✕ 1 mug of cooked sweet potato cubes
- ✕ 1 courgette, thinly sliced

FOR TEXTURES/SPRINKLES (CHOOSE FROM)

- ✕ 1 heaped tbsp toasted pine nuts
- ✕ Crushed walnuts
- ✕ 1 heaped tsp za'atar
- ✕ Pinch of dried oregano
- ✕ Pinch of chilli flakes
- ✕ Fresh basil leaves
- ✕ Fresh parsley leaves
- ✕ Rocket leaves
- ✕ A glug of extra virgin olive oil

GO VEGGIE OR VEGAN:
Simply choose veggie or vegan elements for your pie, to make it vegan use vegan puff pastry and glaze with non-dairy milk.

1. Preheat a baking sheet in the oven at 200°C/180°C fan/Gas Mark 6.
2. Unroll the pastry, leaving it on the parchment paper. Leaving about a 2cm border all around, spread over your flavour base, then layer with a mixture of your choice of toppings. Fold over the border, pleating where necessary, to create an oval-shaped tart; a rustic-look edging is entirely acceptable.

3. Brush the pastry border with the beaten egg, drizzle a little olive oil over the toppings and pop onto the heated baking sheet and into the oven. Bake for about 40 minutes until the border is golden and the toppings look slightly golden and crisp. Sprinkle over your chosen textures and sprinkles, slice up and serve.

THE BASE

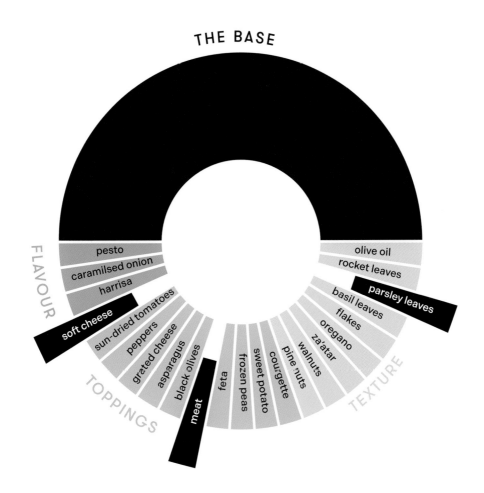

FLAVOUR
- pesto
- caramilsed onion
- harrisa
- soft cheese

TOPPINGS
- sun-dried tomatoes
- peppers
- grated cheese
- asparagus
- black olives
- meat
- feta
- frozen peas
- sweet potato
- courgette
- pine nuts
- walnuts

TEXTURE
- olive oil
- rocket leaves
- parsley leaves
- basil leaves
- flakes
- oregano
- za'atar

CURRY
IN A HURRY

SERVES 4 · 30 MIN · VE

This is a lovely little formula for you, if you like (and I highly recommend) keeping curry pastes around the kitchen. Between that and a tin of coconut milk, you have the canvas of a simple, easy-to-vary recipe (switch up the curry paste to switch up the flavour!) in which to throw your stashes of protein, veg and any leftovers that may need using up. Note the instructions on when to add the ingredients.

FOR THE BASE

2–4 heaped tbsp curry paste, depending on how strong/spicy you want it
400ml tin of coconut milk
1 mug of boiling water

FOR THE PROTEIN (CHOOSE FROM)

✕ 1–2 mugs of frozen/fresh/cooked chicken strips
✕ 1–2 mugs of frozen/fresh prawns/shellfish
✕ 2–4 fish fillets, snipped into bite-size chunks
✕ 400g firm tofu, snipped into bite-size chunks
✕ 400g tin of chickpeas, drained

FOR THE VEG (CHOOSE FROM)

✕ 1 mug of frozen mixed veg
✕ Leftover raw or cooked veg (sweetcorn, peas, aubergine, cauliflower and sweet potato all work well), broken or snipped into small pieces

TO SERVE AND ELEVATE (CHOOSE AS MANY AS YOU LIKE)

✕ Basmati rice or naan bread, to serve
✕ Toasted almonds
✕ Coriander leaves
✕ Lime wedges
✕ Toasted coconut flakes
✕ Lime pickle
✕ Mango chutney
✕ Chopped chillies

GO VEGGIE OR VEGAN:
Simply choose veggie or vegan elements for your curry!

1. Fry the curry paste in a large saucepan over a medium heat, stirring often, until the aromas are released; this will take a couple minutes.
2. Add the coconut milk and the mug of water along with your choice of protein, veg and leftovers. Increase the heat to bring the curry to the boil, then immediately reduce to the lowest simmer and cook until all the ingredients are cooked and piping hot through.
3. The rule here is to add any raw ingredients first; raw larger veg like sweet potato will take about 20 minutes or so to be cooked through, whereas raw chicken strips and raw shellfish will only take a maximum of 10 minutes. Stagger the adding of your ingredients so they all finish cooking at the same time, to avoid tough protein. Any pre-cooked ingredients just need to be heated through until piping hot, generally about 5–10 minutes.
4. Serve the curry with steamed basmati rice or naan bread, with whatever additions you fancy to elevate it.

THE BASE

PROTEIN

chicken

prawns

fish fillets

chickpeas

tofu

fozen veg

raw veg

VEG

basmati rice

toasted almonds

coriander

lime wedges

coconut flakes

lime pickle

mango chutney

chopped chillies

SERVE & ELEVATE

TAKE A TIN OF BEANS

SERVES 2 · 15 MIN · VE

I cannot shout loudly enough about this recipe formula. This is my regular lunch go-to as I always have beans in my store cupboard and with the usual kitchen basics – pastes, spices, eggs, citrus and veg drawer – you can always make a meal of it! This is also a wonderful canvas for leftovers. I think the egg on top is an absolute must. Try to stick to one paste, but otherwise add as you see fit.

FOR THE BASE

2 tbsp olive oil
1 spring onion, snipped
2 garlic cloves, crushed
400g tin of white beans or chickpeas
Extra virgin olive oil, for drizzling

FOR THE SPICE (CHOOSE FROM)

- 1 tsp ground cumin
- 1 tsp paprika (smoked or sweet)
- 1 tsp cayenne pepper

FOR THE PASTE (CHOOSE FROM)

- 2 heaped tbsp pesto
- 1 heaped tbsp rose harissa paste
- 1 tbsp chipotle paste
- 1 tbsp gochujang paste
- 1 heaped tbsp jerk paste
- 1 heaped tbsp tahini paste

FOR THE CITRUS (CHOOSE FROM)

- Juice of ½ lemon
- Juice of ½ lime

FOR THE TOPPERS
(CHOOSE FROM AS MANY AS YOU LIKE)

- Large handful of spinach
- ½ block of feta, crumbled
- ½ packet of diced chorizo
- 2 eggs

FOR THE HERBS AND HEAT (CHOOSE FROM)

- ¼ bunch of coriander
- ¼ bunch of parsley
- ¼ bunch of basil
- Pinch of chilli flakes
- Freshly chopped chillies

Crusty bread, to serve

NO WASTE – FRIDGE FORAGE:
A perfect canvas for using up that odd half of tomato or courgette, or the handful of spinach left in the fridge.

GO VEGGIE OR VEGAN:
Simply choose veggie or vegan elements for your bean stew!

1. Heat the oil in a large frying pan over a medium heat, add the spring onion, garlic and spice and soften, stirring often, for a couple minutes.
2. Add the beans, spice paste and citrus with a splash of water and stir well to combine, crushing some of the beans with a wooden spoon. Stir in the spinach if you are using it and allow it to wilt.
3. Make 2 wells in the bean mix and break in the eggs, if using. Sprinkle any toppings over the beans, pop the lid on and cook until the egg whites are cooked but the yolk is still runny. Season to taste, drizzle with a little extra virgin olive oil and top with herbs and sliced chilli, if you wish. Serve with crusty bread.

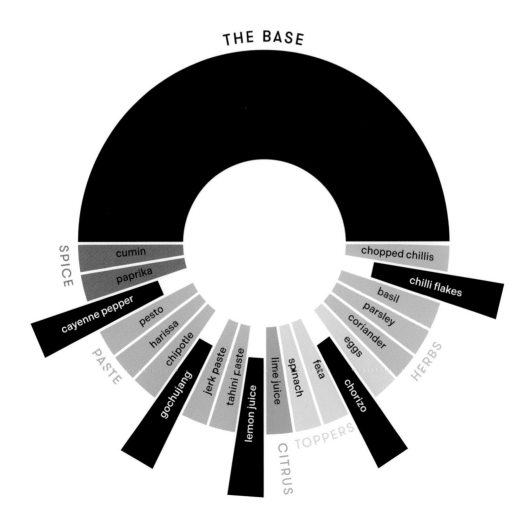

THE BASE

SPICE
cumin
paprika
cayenne pepper

PASTE
pesto
harissa
chipotle
gochujang
jerk paste
tahini paste

CITRUS
lemon juice
lime juice

TOPPERS
spinach
feta
chorizo
eggs

HERBS
coriander
parsley
basil

chopped chillis
chilli flakes

5

JUST ADD PIZAZZ

The kind of easy
je ne sais quoi magic
… actually scrap that,
I know exactly what
these simply clever
recipes do: they create
something special to
elevate your leftover
salads, sarnies, lunches
and all those other
meals we all love.

Mango Jalapeño Jam 146

Chilli Oil 148

Crying Tiger(ish) Sauce 149

Romesco Sauce 150

Smacked Cucumber 151

Rubble Trouble
Crispy Chilli Chickpeas
& Chewy Corn 152
Harissa Nuts & Seeds 152
Chorizo Lemon Crumb 153
Fried Herby Capers 153

Cheatsy Caribbean
(Hot) Pepper Sauce 156

Peri Peri Salt 157

Jalapeño Yoghurt Drizzle 158

Watercress Chilli Salsa 159

Quirky Croutons
Coconut & Lime Bread 160
Chilli Tortilla 160
Parmesan & Oregano Bread 161
Za'atar Pitta 161

MANGO JALAPEÑO JAM

2 soft ripe mangoes, peeled and stoned

1 heaped tbsp jarred jalapeños

10 tbsp jalapeño jar juice

Juice of 1 lemon

1 mug of caster sugar

½ mug of cider vinegar

This is a twist on chilli jam that you will want to have ready to smear, smoosh and dollop over everything. It is especially fab on cheese sandwiches and toasties!

1. Pop the mango flesh and jalapeños into a food processor and blitz until you have a yellow pulp with green flecks.
2. Scrape into a medium saucepan, add the remaining ingredients and bring to the boil. Keep the boil rolling and cook for about 30 minutes, stirring often, until the jam is thick and sticky. Allow to cool a little before transferring into a sterilised jar. Let cool completely then store in the fridge for up to a month.

ELEVATE IT:
Sandwiches, eggs, cheese and charcuterie, toasties, meats and roasted veg.

CHILLI OIL

MAKES 500ML | 10 MIN | VE

1½ mugs of vegetable oil
5 tbsp chilli flakes
2 long dried red chillies

Chilli oil. I think you know what to do with this. This version is stripped back so it works on EVERYTHING! Use it on rice and noodle dishes, such as Lazy Laksa or Fried Rice Mathematics (see pages 106 and 124) as well as on pizzas, pasta, toasties or salads.

1. Pop all the ingredients into a saucepan and set over a medium-low heat, swirling for 5 minutes (don't let it smoke or bubble madly), until the oil is infused with the chilli. Set aside to cool to room temperature.
2. Decant into a sterilised bottle or jar and leave to infuse for a week (if you can wait that long . . .). Seal and store in a dark cupboard for up to 6 months.

ELEVATE IT:
Salad, soups, rice bowls, pastas, sandwiches, literally everything!

CRYING TIGER(ISH) SAUCE

SERVES 4 · 5 MIN · VE

1 tbsp uncooked rice

1–2 heaped tsp chilli flakes

3 tbsp fish sauce

Juice of 1 lime

2 tbsp caster sugar

1 spring onion, finely snipped

2 tbsp finely snipped coriander

This Thai-inspired sauce is a fiery way to elevate simple salads or cold cuts. Go bold with the chilli flakes if you can, they don't call it crying tiger for nothing!

1. First toast the rice in a dry frying pan over a medium heat until golden, then tip onto a plate to cool. Once cooled, bash in a mortar and pestle (or pop in a spice grinder and blitz) to a coarse dust.
2. Add the ground toasted rice to a bowl with all the remaining ingredients and a pinch of seasoning and mix to combine.
3. Cover and keep in the fridge for up to 4 days.

ELEVATE IT:
Serve as a dipping sauce for grilled or roasted meats, shellfish and veg, or drizzle on salads.

GO VEGGIE OR VEGAN
Substitute the fish sauce for a veggie or vegan alternative.

ROMESCO SAUCE

SERVES 6 · 5 MIN · VE

100g toasted flaked almonds (or toasted hazelnuts)

1 garlic clove

1 jar roasted red peppers (about 300g), drained

1 heaped tsp paprika (smoked, ideally)

½ tsp cayenne pepper

1 tbsp sherry vinegar (or red wine)

4 tbsp olive oil

This Catalan-inspired sauce is the simplest thing to make and really elevates so many dishes. Sometimes I toss it through hot pasta and crumble a little feta over. The world is your oyster with this one.

1. Pop all the ingredients except the olive oil into a food processor and blitz until smooth; I like a creamy but thick sauce. Season to taste, adding a splash more vinegar if you like.
2. Pop into a jar or airtight container and keep in the fridge for up to 5 days.

ELEVATE IT:
Crudités and flatbreads, meats, fish, grilled veg, salads, eggs.

SMACKED CUCUMBER

SERVES 4 · 5 MIN · VE

1 cucumber, ends discarded

1 large garlic clove, crushed

1 heaped tbsp caster sugar

1 tbsp chilli oil (ideally Chinese-style)

3 tbsp white wine vinegar

This is actually finger-licking good: it will take next-day second helpings to another level.

1. Use a rolling pin to carefully smack the cucumber all over until it splits, then snip it into bite-size pieces. Mix together in a bowl with the remaining ingredients and season to taste (it will take a lot of salt and pepper).
2. Leave the flavours to sink in for a few minutes before serving, or cover and keep in the fridge for up to 2 days.

ELEVATE IT:
Stir fries, toasties, rice-based dishes.

RUBBLE TROUBLE

You know when you just need a 'little something' to sprinkle over your soups and salads just to give it that je ne sais quoi? Well, here are four little somethings for you . . .

CRISPY CHILLI CHICKPEAS & CHEWY CORN

400g tin of chickpeas, drained*

150g tin of sweetcorn, drained

1 tbsp paprika (smoked or sweet)

1 tsp cayenne

Zest of 1 lime

2 tbsp olive oil

* Save the chickpea water (aquafaba) to make Black Forest Mousse, page 172)

1. Preheat the oven to 200°C/180°C fan/Gas Mark 6.
2. In a large roasting tin, mix together all the ingredients with a pinch of seasoning. Spread the mixture out into a single layer (you may need to use two trays do to this). Pop the tray into the oven and bake for 40–50 minutes, shaking halfway through, until the chickpeas are crisp and golden (they will continue to harden as they cool). Set aside to cool and season to taste.
3. Store in a jar or airtight container for up to 3 days (you may need to re-crisp in a hot oven for 5 minutes or so).

HARISSA NUTS & SEEDS

5 tbsp mixed nuts

5 tbsp mixed seeds

2 tsp rose harissa paste

1 tsp honey

1. Heat a frying pan over a medium heat, add the nuts and seeds and shake the pan for a couple of minutes to toast. Stir in the harissa and honey or maple syrup, cooking until the nuts and seeds are coated and sticky and aromas fill the air. Season to taste.
2. Set aside to cool. Store in a jar or airtight container for up to 3 days.

CHORIZO
LEMON CRUMB

 SERVES 4 10 MIN

1 cured chorizo ring, skin peeled off, and crumbled

7 heaped tbsp (about 50g) breadcrumbs

Zest of ½ lemon

Juice of 1 lemon

1. Heat the frying pan over a medium heat and add the chorizo, cooking until it crisps up a bit and the oil is released, about 5 minutes. Add the breadcrumbs and lemon zest and juice in the last couple of minutes or so. Stir and season to taste.
2. Store in a jar or airtight container for a couple of days (you may need to re-crisp in a hot oven for 5 minutes or so).

FRIED HERBY CAPERS

 SERVES 4 25 MIN VE

1 tbsp olive oil

1 small jar of capers (about 100g), drained and patted dry

Zest of ½ lemon

1 tbsp snipped parsley

2 tbsp breadcrumbs

1. Heat the oil in a frying pan over a medium-high heat and add the capers, stirring often until they begin to crisp up. Add the lemon zest, parsley and breadcrumbs at the end and stir until golden, then season to taste.
2. Store in a jar or airtight container for a couple of days (you may need to re-crisp in a hot oven for 5 minutes or so).

Harissa Nuts & Seeds

Fried Herby Capers

Crispy Chilli Chickpeas
& Chewy Corn

Chorizo Lemon Crumb

CHEATSY CARIBBEAN (HOT) PEPPER SAUCE

 MAKES 75ML 5 MIN VE

2 Scotch bonnet peppers, stem removed

3 garlic cloves

3 sprigs of coriander

1/3 mug of white wine vinegar

2 tsp caster sugar

1/2 mango or 1/2 small papaya, deseeded

I wrote a lengthier recipe for pepper sauce in my first cookbook, but this is now my regular go-to. It isn't only about heat; there is a sweetness that comes out too, with the mango or papaya tempering the chilli. Obviously brilliant with Caribbean food . . . but also with so much more, like curries, stir-fries, rice or couscous-based salads and dishes.

1. Blend all the ingredients in a food processor or blender until smooth, then season to taste. The flavours will improve with time, so if you can, be patient!
2. Decant into a sterilised bottle or jar and leave to infuse for a week (do try and wait this long ☺). Seal and store in a dark cupboard for up to 6 months.

ELEVATE IT:
EVERYTHING!

PERI PERI SALT

SERVES 7 · 5 MIN · VE

2 tsp garlic powder

4 tsp sweet smoked paprika

3 tsp sea salt flakes

2 tsp caster sugar

2 tsp dried oregano

1 tsp cayenne pepper

This is pure magic dust. For me it is all about generously sprinkling over oven chips, roast potatoes or wedges, but really, it can work on meat and veggies – sprinkle over your Chilli Thyme Roasted Tomatoes & Feta (see page 72), Anytime Breakfast Smash (see page 75), Hasty Hollandaise (see page 193), or even your Mindless Mash in Minutes (see page 190).

1. Mix together all the ingredients. Store in a jar or airtight container alongside your spices and herbs.

ELEVATE IT:
Meat, fish, roasted veg, eggs, chips, salads and soups.

JALAPEÑO YOGHURT DRIZZLE

SERVES 4 · 5 MINS · V · VE

4 heaped tbsp natural yoghurt

1 large garlic clove, peeled

2 tbsp jarred jalapeños, plus 1 tbsp of liquid from the jar

1 sprig of coriander

This accidental discovery, purely hashed together to use up the last of a jar of jalapeños and some yoghurt, has been a 'Eureka' moment. One my favourite ways to enjoy this is as a dip for charred Tenderstem broccoli. So good!

1. Pulse the ingredients in a food processor or blender and season well. Don't worry about it being smooth, but it should be a drizzling consistency. Store in a covered jar or airtight container in the fridge for 4 days.

ELEVATE IT:
Dipping sauces, sandwiches, meat and fish, rice dishes, burritos (see page 49), soups, salads.

GO VEGAN:
Substitute the natural yoghurt for a vegan alternative.

WATERCRESS CHILLI SALSA

 SERVES 6 5 MINS VE

1 small bag (about 80g) of watercress

1 small bunch (about 25g) of parsley

1 small bunch (about 25g) of coriander

1 red chilli

1 tbsp capers

½ mug of extra virgin olive oil

1 garlic clove, crushed

Juice of 1 lemon

I love this recipe. It is heaven-sent for using up sad salad – try it with rocket or spinach if you have any that needs using up. You can remove the chilli seeds for a milder salsa.

1. Pop the watercress, herbs, chilli and capers with a little of the oil into a food processor and pulse until everything is finely chopped. Stir in the remaining oil, then the garlic and lemon juice, and season to taste.
2. Store in a jar or airtight container in the fridge for up to 5 days.

ELEVATE IT:
Cold meat, charcuterie, cooked fish, eggs, sandwiches and roasted veg, try with chicken traybakes, Picnic Loaf (see page 82), Veg Hero Burgers (see page 81).

NO WASTE – FRIDGE FORAGE:
Perfect for any sad dark salad leaves or wilting herbs.

QUIRKY CROUTONS

These really need no introduction! I have gone a bit zany with flavour combinations so you won't get bored. The Coconut & Lime Bread is fabulous on dals, Chilli Tortilla on tomato-based soups, Za'atar Pitta with mezze and dips and the Parmesan & Oregano Bread on tomato and mozzarella salads. But really, there is no prescribed way to enjoy these.

COCONUT & LIME BREAD

 SERVES 4 25 MIN VE

4 thick slices of bread (stale works well!), torn into small bite-size chunks

3 heaped tbsp coconut oil

2 tsp garlic granules

Grated zest of 1 lime

1. Preheat the oven to 200°C/180°C fan/Gas Mark 6.
2. Pop all the ingredients as well as a pinch of seasoning into a freezer bag (or bowl), seal and shake well to fully coat the bread chunks (or mix well in a bowl). Tip out onto a baking sheet and pop into the oven for about 15–20 minutes until crispy and golden, giving a shake halfway through. Remove and set aside to cool.
3. Store in a jar or airtight container and use within 7 days (they may need a re-crisp in a hot oven for a few minutes).

CHILLI TORTILLA

 SERVES 4 30 MIN VE

4 tortillas or wraps, torn into bite-size pieces

4 tbsp olive oil

2 tbsp Cajun seasoning

1. Preheat the oven to 200°C/180°C fan/Gas Mark 6.
2. Pop all the ingredients as well as a pinch of seasoning into a freezer bag (or bowl), seal and shake well to coat the tortilla pieces (or mix well in a bowl). Tip out onto a baking sheet and pop into the oven for about 20–25 minutes until crispy and golden, giving a shake halfway through. Remove and set aside to cool.
3. Store in a jar or an airtight container and use within 7 days (they may need a re-crisp in a hot oven for a few minutes).

PARMESAN & OREGANO BREAD

4 thick slices of bread (stale works well!), torn into small bite-size chunks

4 tbsp extra virgin olive oil

3 heaped tbsp grated Parmesan cheese or Grana Padano (or use a veggie or vegan alternative)

1½ tbsp dried oregano

1. Preheat the oven to 200°C/180°C fan/Gas Mark 6.
2. Pop all the ingredients as well as a pinch of seasoning into a freezer bag (or bowl), seal and shake well to coat the bread (or mix well in a bowl). Tip out onto a baking sheet and pop into the oven for about 15–20 minutes until crispy and golden, giving a shake halfway through.
3. Remove and set aside to cool. Store in a jar or an airtight container and use within 7 days (they may need a re-crisp in a hot oven for a few minutes).

ZA'ATAR PITTA

4 pitta breads, torn into bite-size pieces

4 tbsp extra virgin olive oil

2 tbsp za'atar

1. Preheat the oven to 200°C/180°C fan/Gas Mark 6.
2. Pop all the ingredients as well as a pinch of seasoning into a freezer bag (or bowl), seal and shake well to coat the pitta (or mix well in a bowl). Tip out onto a baking sheet and pop into the oven for about 20–25 minutes until crispy and golden, giving a shake halfway through. Remove and set aside to cool.
3. Store in a jar or airtight container and use within 7 days (they may need a re-crisp in a hot oven for a few minutes).

Coconut & Lime Bread

Parmesan &
Oregano Bread

Chilli Tortilla

Za'atar Pitta

6

NO SWEAT SWEETS

Let's not make desserts a drudgery, instead try your hand at the most divine cheatsy sweetsies.

ONE PAN COOKIE

SERVES 4-6 · 35 MIN · V

½ block of softened unsalted butter (125g), plus extra for greasing

½ mug of (ideally golden) caster sugar (100g)

1 large egg

2 tsp vanilla extract or vanilla bean paste

1 mug of plain flour (filled right to the top, not packed down)

1 tsp baking powder

½ mug of dark or milk chocolate chips/smarties

½ tsp sea salt flakes

Vanilla ice cream, to serve

Oh my days. You know those times when you are hit with desire for a gooey, melty chocolate chip cookie, a craving that can't be curbed by anything from a packet? Well now you have the recipe. It's a great sharer. You could even make double the dough and pop half into the freezer for another time (when you want a sugar pick-me-up with even less elbow grease)! Pop a scoop of ice cream into the middle when it comes out of the oven. Bliss.

1. Preheat the oven to 190°C/170°C fan/Gas Mark 5 and lightly butter a heavy-based ovenproof frying pan.
2. Beat together the butter and sugar until light and fluffy, then beat in the egg and vanilla. Finally fold in the flour, baking powder and chocolate chips along with the sea salt flakes. Bring together with your hands to make a large ball of cookie dough.
3. Spoon and push down the cookie dough into the greased pan, ensuring the dough is squished up to all the edges of the pan. Pop it into the oven and bake for about 30 minutes until lightly golden on the edges but still a little gooey in the centre. Top with a large scoop of vanilla ice cream and enjoy.

BOOZY BANOFFEE GALETTE

SERVES 4-6 · 40 MIN · V

1 sheet of ready-rolled puff pastry

4 heaped tbsp salted caramel sauce (or dulce de leche)

3 bananas, peeled and sliced into 1-cm rounds

Generous splash of good-quality dark rum (optional)

1 small bar (about 45g) of good-quality hazelnut dark chocolate, broken into small shards

1 tsp ground cinnamon

1 beaten egg, to glaze

Ice cream, whipped cream or double cream, to serve

A fancier version of a banoffee pie, perhaps? Don't let the word 'galette' put you off; it's simply a very rustically put together, freeform pie. Perfect for throwing together with the kids (and eating with them too, if you leave the splash of rum out!). If you've got some ripe bananas that need eating up, this is a welcome alternative to banana bread.

1. Preheat the oven to 200°C/180°C fan/Gas Mark 6 and put a baking sheet inside to heat up too.
2. Trim one side of the pastry rectangle so you end up with a square shape. Keeping the pastry on its parchment paper, spoon a heaped tablespoon of the salted caramel sauce onto the middle, smoothing it into a 20-cm circle. Add a layer of banana slices, starting in the middle and going round in a swirl pattern.
3. Lift and fold the edges of the pastry up to form a small rim (about 1cm) that surrounds your banana and caramel centre. Drizzle over another couple of tablespoons of salted caramel sauce as well as the rum (if using) and sprinkle over the shards of hazelnut chocolate and the cinnamon. Glaze the rim with the beaten egg.
4. Pop the galette, still on its paper, onto the heated baking sheet and into the oven for 25–30 minutes until the pastry is crisp and golden and the bananas have caramelised. Serve hot, with extra salted caramel sauce and ice cream, whipped cream or double cream.

NO WASTE – FRIDGE FORAGE:
Perfect for overripe bananas.

BLACK FOREST MOUSSE

2 large bars of good-quality dark chocolate (200g), broken into small pieces

Aquafaba from 1 x 400g tin of chickpeas

3 tbsp caster sugar

Pinch of sea salt flakes

4 heaped tbsp of jarred or tinned cherries in kirsch or syrup

This is how I use my aquafaba – that's the chickpea water from a tin if you didn't know! You do have to be patient when whisking into stiff peaks, but it is so worth it. The combination of dark chocolate and kirsch (or syrup) is exceptional, with the whipped 'cream' and grated chocolate elevating it to a Black Forest taste sensation.

1. Melt the chocolate in short bursts on high in the microwave, stirring often. Alternatively put into a heatproof bowl set over a pan of barely simmering water, and melt, making sure the bowl isn't touching the water. Leave to cool a little.
2. Meanwhile, whisk the aquafaba and sugar together with a hand-held electric whisk until it forms really stiff peaks – this will take about 10 minutes. Be patient! Fold in the cooled chocolate along with a generous pinch of sea salt flakes. Don't over fold, otherwise the mousse will lose its airiness.
3. Add a tablespoon of cherries, along with a little kirsch or syrup into the base of four serving glasses (ideally clear, for effect), then divide and layer over the mousse. Pop in the fridge to chill for a couple hours before serving.

ELEVATE IT:
Top with whipped cream and grated chocolate just before serving.

NO WASTE – FRIDGE FORAGE:
Perfect for leftover aquafaba.

GO VEGAN:
Just ensure your dark chocolate is vegan (dark chocolate with a high percentage of cocoa solids will tend to be vegan).

CARROT CAKE PANCAKES

1 mug of self-raising flour (about 180g)

2 tbsp brown sugar

1 tsp ground cinnamon, plus extra for dusting

1 tsp bicarbonate of soda

1 egg

½ mug of milk (about 150ml)

1 large carrot, grated

Butter, for frying

4 tbsp cream cheese

4 tbsp maple syrup

These are a lovely alternative to your usual pancakes – quite often I'll whip up a quick batch of these as a dessert or afternoon treat. And what do you know, we've managed to squeeze a veg into a sweet!

1. Whisk together the flour, sugar, spice and bicarbonate of soda together. Then whisk in the egg and milk and finally, the grated carrot.
2. Heat ½ tablespoon of butter in a large frying pan over a medium heat. Once the butter begins to foam, pour in a couple of tablespoons of the batter and cook for about 2 minutes until bubbles begin to pop up on the surface of the pancake. Then carefully flip it over and cook for another couple minutes. Set aside, keep warm and repeat with the remaining batter.
3. Mix together the cream cheese and maple syrup until a loose cream is formed. Dollop onto the pancakes, along with a dusting of cinnamon.

ELEVATE IT:
Top with crumbled walnuts, raisins.

NO WASTE – FRIDGE FORAGE:
Perfect for using up crinkly carrots.

FROZEN PEANUT BUTTER CUPS

SERVES 12 | 10 MIN | VE

3 heaped tbsp coconut oil (or softened butter), plus extra for greasing

5 heaped tbsp peanut butter

6 digestive biscuits, blitzed or bashed in a tea-towel until finely crumbed

Pinch of sea salt flakes

1 large bar of dark chocolate (100–150g)

This was created during the first lockdown and we have never looked back; there is always a bag of them in our freezer, ready to go. Such a treat and great to make with the kids.

1. Grease a 12-hole cupcake tray (or use a 24-hole mini cupcake tray).
2. Melt the chocolate in short bursts on high in the microwave, stirring often. Alternatively put into a heatproof bowl set over a pan of barely simmering water, and melt, making sure the bowl isn't touching the water. Leave to cool a little. Mix together the coconut oil, peanut butter and biscuit crumbs with a generous pinch of sea salt flakes.
3. Divide the mixture between the holes of your cupcake tray, pushing the mixture right down into the holes with the back of a spoon and making it as level as possible.
4. Carefully spoon over the dark chocolate and pop into a freezer. Once frozen solid, pop out the cups and enjoy, or store in a resealable freezer bag in the freezer.

INDIAN-SPICED SWEET CARROT PUDDING

SERVES 4 · 45 MIN · V

4 large carrots (500g), blitzed in a food processor or grated

½ mug of condensed milk

½ mug of whole milk

1 heaped tbsp ground cardamom

1 heaped tbsp ghee (or unsalted butter)

1 tbsp sugar

3 heaped tbsp raisins or sultanas

3 heaped tbsp flaked almonds

Loosely based on an Indian sweet (halwa), as soon as I made this I was hooked. Usually made with red carrots, this cheatsy version uses bog-standard (but beautiful) regular orange carrots. The spice makes it a comforting treat that is very unusual so do give it a try. Totally blasphemous, but I really enjoy this with custard! It also makes a lovely afternoon treat.

1. Put the carrot, condensed milk, whole milk and cardamom into a small saucepan, bring to the boil and stir regularly until the mixture is really thick, with most of the liquid evaporated, about 20 minutes.
2. Melt the butter in a small frying pan, add the sugar and cook over a high heat until the butter is frothy, then tip in the carrot mixture and fry for about 15 minutes, continuously stirring, until the mixture has caramelised and darkened.
3. Finally add the raisins and almonds and cook for another 5 minutes, stirring often, until the mixture is sticky and thick with no liquid. Enjoy hot or cold.

ELEVATE IT:
Serve with vanilla ice cream, custard or thick yoghurt.

NO WASTE – FRIDGE FORAGE:
Perfect for using up crinkly carrots.

ALMOST INSTANT LAVA CAKE TWO WAYS

SERVES 4 · 15 MIN · V

Butter, for greasing

4 large chocolate muffins

1 large bar (100g) of chocolate, broken into smaller pieces

4 tbsp (salted) caramel sauce

Ice cream, to serve

OR

4 large blueberry muffins

1 large bar (100g) of white chocolate, broken into smaller pieces

Ice cream, to serve

Now this is really the best way to take a shop-bought muffin and turn it into pure, gooey-centred decadence. Forget baking from scratch – with this cheat you can be enjoying a showstopper in 15 minutes. There is also nothing wrong with using ready-made caramel sauce; if you can't find a salted version, simply add a pinch of sea salt flakes and you are good to go.

1. Preheat the oven to 200°C/180°C fan/Gas Mark 6 and grease 4 large ramekins with butter.

2. Pop the muffins into the ramekins, then poke a hole in the middle of each muffin and hide a quarter of the chocolate inside. If using chocolate muffins, pop a tablespoon of the salted caramel on top of the muffin. Cover with foil, tenting it over so it doesn't touch the top of the muffin.

3. Place in the oven for about 10 minutes until the muffin is hot and the chocolate centre is runny. Carefully remove the foil and serve immediately with a scoop of ice cream on top.

LEMON EASECAKE

SERVES 4 | 10 MIN | V

10 ginger snap biscuits

4 heaped tbsp butter, melted

280g tub of cream cheese

7 heaped tbsp caster sugar

Zest and juice of 1 lemon

4 heaped tbsp lemon curd, or passionfruit curd

I love a cheesecake and this has to be the simplest 'version' there is. It tastes fantastic and can look really spectacular, especially if you elevate it. No need for fussy springform tins here.

1. Blitz the biscuits in a food processor, or wrap the biscuits in a tea towel and bash with a rolling pin until you have a coarse crumb like consistency. Mix the crumbs with the butter, then divide the buttery biscuit crumb between 4 serving bowls or glasses (clear glass will give the best effect), pressing it into the base of the glass with the back of a spoon.

2. Beat the cream cheese, caster sugar, lemon zest and juice together until smooth and creamy. Carefully dollop over the biscuit base, being careful not to touch the base with your spoon as it may mess up the biscuit layer, then spoon over the lemon curd. Leave to chill in the fridge for half an hour before enjoying.

ELEVATE IT:
Just before serving, top with fresh passionfruit, snipped mint leaves, extra lemon zest.

STICKY ROAST PEACHES

 SERVES 4 30 MIN V VE

4 ripe peaches, halved and stone removed

4 tbsp Amaretto (optional)

4 heaped tbsp runny honey

2 tsp ground cinnamon

Small pinch of sea salt flakes

4 amaretti biscuits, partially crumbled

4 mint leaves, torn

Ice cream, cream or yoghurt, to serve

Ok, so you need to halve the peaches with a knife, but then that is as hard as it gets. This simple sweet treat looks and feels incredibly sophisticated, but it is also a clever way to make the most of peaches that are a little unripe and not so sweet, as well as – conversely – a little overripe too. Leave out the Amaretto if this is for kids.

1. Preheat the oven to 200°C/180°C fan/Gas Mark 6.
2. Pop the peaches into a roasting tin, cut side up. Drizzle over the Amaretto (if using) and the honey, then sprinkle over the cinnamon and a tiny pinch of sea salt flakes. Pop into the oven to roast for 20–25 minutes until golden and sticky.
3. Scatter over the crumbled amaretti and mint leaves and serve immediately with ice cream, cream or yoghurt.

GO VEGAN:
Substitute the honey for maple syrup and use vegan amaretti biscuits.

NO WASTE – FRIDGE FORAGE:
This works with both hard peaches or overripe squidgy ones!

7

FAVOURITE
BASICS

A handful of
simple recipes and
techniques that
you'll probably find
yourself coming back
to as a basic starting
point for your meals.

QUICK TOMATO SAUCE

SERVES 2-4 · 12 MIN · VE

1 tbsp olive oil

2 garlic cloves, crushed

1 heaped tsp oregano

400g tin of chopped tomatoes

2 tbsp extra virgin olive oil

Unless I'm grabbing a jar of ready-made from the supermarket, this is my go-to tomato sauce: quick, tasty and perfect for pastas. If I want to use this for a pizza, I simmer for longer to allow it to thicken up to a really thick base. If you have basil leaves lying around throw them in with the oregano. And you can always double the batch and freeze half for another use!

1. Heat the olive oil in a saucepan over a medium heat and add the garlic and oregano along with a pinch of salt. Stir until the aromas hit you.
2. Add the chopped tomatoes and some more seasoning and simmer for 10 minutes until rich and a little thicker. Finally stir in the extra virgin olive oil.

QUICK POTATO & CHICKPEA CURRY SAUCE

 SERVES 4 20 MIN V VE

2 heaped tbsp butter

1 onion, peeled and pulsed in a food processor until roughly chopped

3 garlic cloves, crushed

2 heaped tbsp curry powder

400g tin of chopped tomatoes

1 tin of peeled new potatoes, about 500g

400g tin of chickpeas

The quickest curry sauce from scratch ever! This may be the first time you have ever used tinned potatoes so I'll say to you now – what have you been waiting for? They were made for throwing into curries, soups, stews and casseroles – basically anything rich and saucy that they can absorb flavour from. This is a fabulous basic curry in which you can throw leftovers, odds and ends and freezer bits in, but it's also pretty great by itself with rice or naan bread.

1. Heat the butter in a saucepan over a medium heat, then add the onion and brown for about 10 minutes, stirring regularly.
2. Add the garlic and curry powder and stir until the aromas hit you, then add the chopped tomatoes, a mug of boiling water, the potatoes and chickpeas and continue to cook until the ingredients are piping hot through, crushing a few potatoes into the sauce to thicken it as you stir. Season to taste.

ELEVATE IT:
Top with chopped chillies, fresh coriander, coconut flakes.

NO WASTE – FRIDGE FORAGE:
If you have leftover cooked potato – roasted, boiled or baked – this is perfect for using it up.

GO VEGAN:
Just use vegan butter.

CHICKEN OR FISH FREEZER STRIPPERS

8–12 skinless and boneless chicken thighs, or 4 small breasts or fish fillets

FOR JERK CHICKEN STRIPPERS
1–2 heaped tbsp jerk paste (depending on how spicy you want it)

FOR MEDITERRANEAN CHICKEN STRIPPERS
4 tbsp olive oil

2 tsp ground cumin

4 tsp dried oregano

2 tsp paprika (smoked or sweet)

1 large garlic clove, peeled and crushed

Zest and juice of 1 lemon

Yes, I know that this is very *Ice Kitchen*, but this technique is too handy a shortcut (and great for avoiding waste), that it was imperative for me to include it! By prepping chicken this way, you can use it straight from frozen (completely safely) and it will cook in no time. Perfect to throw into curries, sauces, stews, casseroles or stir-fries. Even better, you can marinate some portions of your raw chicken or fish in the freezer so that you have flavourbomb proteins ready to go, cutting out any marinating times that a recipe may call for!

1. Use kitchen scissors to cut the chicken or fish fillets into 2-cm thick strips. Open-freeze on a tray until solid then pop into a resealable freezer bag.
2. To make marinated jerk chicken strippers, pop the chicken and jerk paste into a resealable freezer bag, seal well and massage the paste into the meat. Separate the strips and lay flat on a tray to freeze so that the strips freeze individually.
3. To make marinated Mediterranean chicken strippers, pop the ingredients into a resealable freezer bag along with a pinch of seasoning, seal well and massage the marinade into the meat. Separate the strips and lay flat on a tray to freeze so that the strips freeze individually.
4. Once frozen you can pop into a resealable freezer bag and store upright if you fancy.

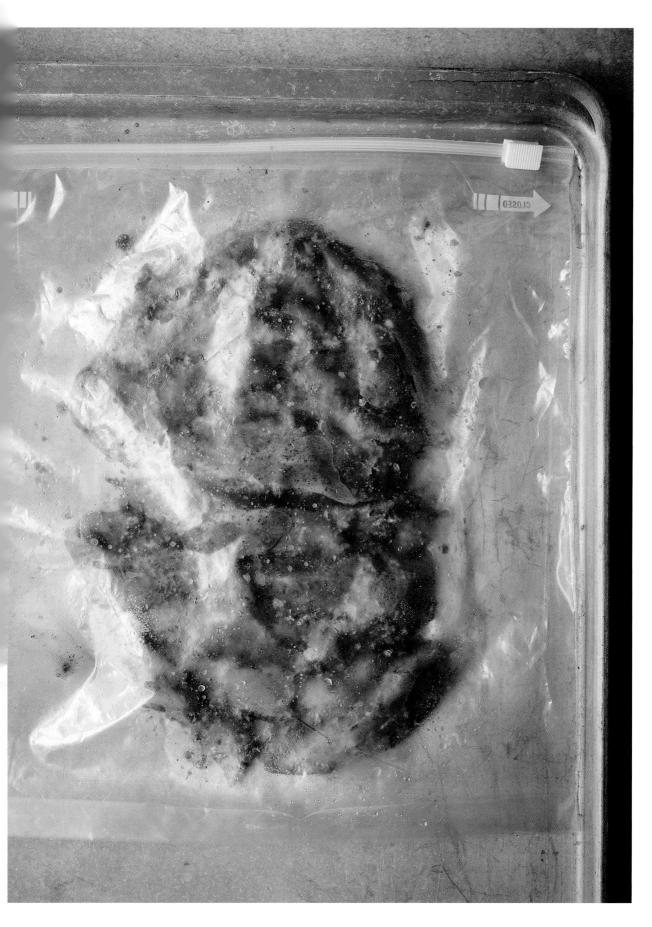

MINDLESS MASH
IN MINUTES

SERVES 4 · 10 MIN · V

½ mug of milk (ideally whole)

4 tbsp butter

2 tins of peeled new potatoes, about 500g a tin

Ready in a jiffy and beautifully enriched with milk and butter, who cares that the potatoes are from a tin? This is a perfect go-to for topping pies, to serve with sausages or any other way you love to use mash. This freezes beautifully too. It really is a smart way to be mindless.

1. In a large saucepan over a medium heat, heat the milk with the butter until hot, being careful to not let the milk scorch. Add the potatoes and mash in gradually, then beat with a wooden spoon until hot through. Season to taste.

FROZEN PEASTO

SERVES 4 · 10 MIN · V

1 garlic clove, crushed

3 tbsp pine nuts

1 mug of frozen peas, blanched in hot water for a couple minutes to defrost

Juice of ½ lemon

⅓ mug of grated Parmesan cheese

4 tbsp extra virgin olive oil

I bet if there is one thing you always have in your freezer it's going to be peas! With a few other basic fridge and store cupboard ingredients, you can blitz those peas into more than just a side dish. Let this take the place of regular pesto, pile it onto pasta, chicken and fish or serve with eggs. If you have basil to hand, throw that in with the peas for something a little extra.

1. Blitz the garlic and pine nuts in a food processor until finely chopped.
2. Add the peas, lemon juice and Parmesan and blitz until you get your desired consistency, then stir in the extra virgin olive oil. Season to taste and add a splash of water if you want it a little looser.

GO VEGGIE:
Use a vegetarian Parmesan replacement.

MAYO FOR MORONS

SERVES
6

5
MIN

VE

3 tbsp aquafaba
1 garlic clove, crushed
Generous pinch of sea salt
A little less than 1 mug vegetable oil
2 tbsp cider or white wine vinegar
1 tbsp Dijon mustard
2 tbsp rose harissa (optional)

Now, I'm not calling you a moron, I'm just saying that no one can go wrong with this blended mayo that is all creaminess and no fussiness. The best bit is that it uses up the aquafaba from tins of chickpeas too, so it's bang on our waste-free agenda. Freeze leftover aquafaba in ice-cube trays to make more when you need it (the mayo itself doesn't freeze so well).

1. Blitz together all the ingredients, with a generous pinch of seasoning, in a blender or with a hand-held blender until thick and creamy. You can store this in the fridge in an airtight container for 1 week.
2. For a twist, mix the rose harissa into the finished mayo.

HASTY HOLLANDAISE

 SERVES 4 5 MIN V

FOR A BASIC HOLLANDAISE
4 egg yolks*
5 tbsp soured cream
4 tbsp butter
Juice of ½ lemon, plus extra to taste

TWIST 1: JALAPEÑO HOLLANDAISE
3 tbsp jarred jalapeño 'juice'

TWIST 2: 'BEARNAISE'
3 tbsp tarragon leaves

TWIST 3: CHIPOTLE HOLLANDAISE
1 tbsp chipotle paste

* Freeze the whites! Just put into a plastic container, making sure you label it clearly with the number of egg whites. Defrosted egg whites make excellent meringues.

Hollandaise will become an everyday option when you realise just how easy it is to cheat it! It's very simple to twist this by adding pinches of spices, chopped herbs and tablespoons of pastes. It's obviously made for eggs, but works beautifully with potatoes, sausages and steaks.

1. Pop the basic ingredients into a saucepan, set over a low heat and whisk continuously until thick and rich.
2. Season to taste, adding more lemon juice if you fancy.

Twist 1
Add the jalapeño 'juice' with the other ingredients in step 1.

Twist 2
Add the tarragon with the other ingredients in step 1, then blitz with a hand-held blender or in a food processor until the tarragon is finely chopped into the hollandaise.

Twist 3
Add the chipotle paste with the other ingredients in step 1.

INSTANT CRUMBING TECHNIQUE FOR GOUJONS & FINGERS

5 MIN

Skinless chicken breasts or thigh fillet (or use skinless fish fillets)
Breadcrumbs (panko will give a crunchier crumb)

If the thought of egg, flour, breadcrumbs and the inevitable mess that that process normally ensues has you running a mile . . . this is for you. When I say instant, I mean one-step; it does the job quite sufficiently, minimising all that mess too. It's not one for freezing but is great for crumbing and using immediately.

1. Pop the chicken on a chopping board and place a sheet of parchment paper or silicone sheet on top. Flatten the chicken by pounding it with a rolling pin (if you're crumbing fish, just gently flatten it, otherwise the fish will disintegrate) and sprinkle a little seasoning on both sides.
2. Firmly press the breadcrumbs into the chicken with your hand, then gently flip over and press more onto the other side.

APPENDIX

APPENDIX 1:
VEGGIE OR VEGAN

Here is a list of recipes that are already veggie or vegan, or can easily be made so with a few substitutions, as detailed in the individual recipes.

Vegan

1. Forest Bolognese
2. Crispy Tofu Asian Loaded Fries
3. Hoisin Mushroom Pancakes
4. Mumbai Roasted Potato
5. Bready Beans
6. Hasty (& Tasty) Hummus
7. Solve All Curry Sauce
8. Jalapeño Mango Jam
9. Chilli Oil
10. Romesco Sauce
11. Smacked Cucumber
12. Rubble Trouble: Crispy Chilli Chickpeas & Chewy Corn
13. Rubble Trouble: Harissa Nuts & Seeds
14. Rubble Trouble: Fried Herby Capers
15. Cheatsy Caribbean (Hot) Pepper Sauce
16. Peri Peri Salt
17. Watercress Chilli Salsa
18. Quirky Croutons: Coconut & Lime Bread
19. Quirky Croutons: Chilli Tortilla
20. Quirky Croutons: Za'atar Pitta
21. Frozen Peanut Butter Cups
22. Black Forest Mousse
23. Quick Tomato Sauce
24. Mayo for Morons

Vegan Option

1. Nearly Numbing Noodles
2. Firecracker Quesadillas
3. Harissa Roast Gnocchi Bake
4. Chilli Con Sausage
5. Mexican Brunch Burrito
6. Kind of Keema Lamb Pau
7. Sausage & Mushroom Ragu
8. Corn Dumpling Soup
9. Chilli Thyme Roasted Tomatoes & Feta
10. Veg Hero Burgers
11. Picnic Loaf
12. Masala Naan Bread Pizza
13. One Pott-anesca
14. Asian Pork Lettuce Wraps
15. Bloody Mary Pasta
16. Sa(d)lad Pesto
17. Hansel & Gretel Spaghetti
18. Lazy Laksa
19. Bang Bang Rainbow Salad
20. Creamy Harissa Feta & Minty Pea Topping
21. Wrapper's Delight
22. Build Me Up Buttercup Board
23. Focacciazza
24. Fried Rice Mathematics
25. Peanut & Ginger Sauce
26. Pimped Packet Noodle Ramen
27. Make a Pie of it
28. Curry in a Hurry
29. Take a Tin of Beans
30. Crying Tiger(ish) Sauce
31. Jalapeno Yoghurt Drizzle
32. Quirky Croutons: Parmesan & Oregano Bread
33. Sticky Roast Peaches
34. Quick Potato & Chickpea Curry Sauce

Veggie

1. Nearly Numbing Noodles
2. Buffalo Roast Cauli 'Potato' Salad
3. Firecracker Quesadillas
4. Forest Bolognese
5. Harissa Roast Gnocchi Bake
6. Cheatballs
7. Crispy Tofu Asian Loaded Fries
8. Hoisin Mushroom Pancakes
9. Chilli Thyme Roasted Tomatoes & Feta
10. Mumbai Roasted Potato
11. Veg Hero Burgers
12. Masala Naan Bread Pizzas
13. Bready Beans
14. Sriracha Honey Cheese Toastie
15. Crispy Halloumi & Hot Honey
16. Hasty (& Tasty) Hummus
17. Creamy Harissa Feta & Minty Pea Topping
18. Build Me Up Buttercup Board
19. Solve All Curry Sauce
20. Peanut & Ginger Sauce
21. Mango Jalapeno Jam
22. Chilli Oil
23. Romesco Sauce
24. Smacked Cucumber
25. Rubble Trouble: Crispy Chilli Chickpeas & Chewy Corn
26. Rubble Trouble: Harissa Nuts & Seeds
27. Rubble Trouble: Fried Herby Capers
28. Cheatsy Caribbean (Hot) Pepper Sauce
29. Peri Peri Salt
30. Jalapeno Yoghurt Drizzle
31. Watercress Chilli Salsa
32. Quirky Croutons: Coconut & Lime Bread
33. Quirky Croutons: Chilli Tortilla
34. Quirky Croutons: Za'atar Pitta
35. One Pot Cookie
36. Frozen Peanut Butter Cups
37. Black Forest Mousse
38. Carrot Cake Pancakes
39. Indian-spiced Sweet Carrot Pudding
40. Boozy Banoffee Galette
41. Almost Instant Lava Cake Two Ways
42. Lemon Easecake
43. Quick Tomato Sauce
44. Quick Potato & Chickpea Curry Sauce
45. Mindless Mash in Minutes
46. Mayo for Morons
47. Hasty Hollandaise

Veggie Option

1. Chilli Con Sausage
2. Mexican Brunch Burrito
3. Kind of Keema Lamb Pau
4. Cajun Hash Benedict
5. Micro Zap Bibimbap
6. Sausage & Mushroom Ragu
7. Spaghetti Meatballs Traybake
8. Chicken Cobbler
9. Anytime Breakfast Smash
10. Picnic Loaf
11. One Pott-anesca
12. Bloody Mary Pasta
13. Sa(d)lad Pesto
14. Cheatsy Cheese & Chorizo Rough Scones
15. Hansel & Gretel Spaghetti
16. Lazy Laksa
17. Bang Bang Rainbow Salad
18. Wrapper's Delight
19. Focacciazza
20. Fried Rice Mathematics
21. Pimped Packet Noodle Ramen
22. No Stir Risotto
23. No Chop Chopped Salad
24. Make a Pie of it
25. Curry in a Hurry
26. Take a Tin of Beans
27. Crying Tiger(ish) Sauce

APPENDIX 2:
USE UP SAD VEG

Here are some commonly found sad or
past-its-best veg and salad items and
ways in which you can use them.

Mushrooms

- Nearly Numbing Noodles
- Anytime Breakfast Smash
- Veg Hero Burgers
- Mexican Brunch Burrito
- Cheatballs
- Sausage & Mushroom Ragu
- Forest Bolognese
- Chicken Cobbler
- Hoisin Mushroom Pancakes

Spinach

- Nearly Numbing Noodles
- Firecracker Quesadillas
- Anytime Breakfast Smash
- Mexican Brunch Burrito
- Cheatballs
- Cajun Hash Benedict
- Chicken Cobbler
- Hasty (& Tasty) Hummus: Chorizo,
  Spinach & Pepper
- Watercress Chilli Salsa

Carrots

- Veg Hero Burgers
- Carrot Cake Pancakes
- Indian-Spiced Sweet Carrot Pudding

Tomatoes

- Firecracker Quesadillas
- Anytime Breakfast Smash
- Veg Hero Burgers
- Picnic Loaf
- Masala Naan Bread Pizza
- Harissa Roast Gnocchi Bake

Salad (cucumber, rocket or lettuce leaves, pepper)

- Firecracker Quesadillas
- Veg Hero Burgers
- Picnic Loaf
- Harissa Roast Gnocchi Bake
- Watercress Chilli Salsa

Courgette

- Veg Hero Burgers
- Mexican Brunch Burrito
- Cheatballs

Cauliflower

- Buffalo Roast Cauli 'Potato' Salad

Squash/pumpkin

- Mexican Brunch Burrito

Coriander

- Masala Naan Bread Pizza
- Mexican Brunch Burrito
- Nearly Numbing Noodles
- Watercress Chilli Salsa

Parsley

- Inside Out Chicken Kyiv
- Veg Hero Burgers
- Watercress Chilli Salsa

Mint

- Mediterranean Chicken Kebabs
- Masala Naan Bread Pizza

Basil

- Picnic Loaf
- One Pott-anesca
- Forest Bolognese
- Bready Beans

Banana

- Boozy Banoffee Galette

APPENDIX 3:
LOVE YOUR LEFTOVERS

Here are some commonly found cooked kitchen leftovers and recipes in which you can use them up.

Chicken

- Mediterranean Chicken Kebabs
- Firecracker Quesadillas
- Mexican Brunch Burrito
- Coronation Chicken Rice Salad

Pork

- Firecracker Quesadillas
- Mexican Brunch Burrito

Beef

- Firecracker Quesadillas
- Mexican Brunch Burrito

Lamb

- Wrapper's Delight
- Fried Rice Mathematics

Roast Veg

- Mediterranean Chicken Kebabs
- Firecracker Quesadillas
- Mexican Brunch Burrito

Soups

- Quirky Croutons
- Rubble Trouble

Mashed Potato

- Inside Out Chicken Kyiv
- Sausage & Mushroom Ragu
- Cheatballs
- Fish (& Chip) Cakes
- Melting Beef Pot

Rice

- Kind of Keema Lamb Pau
- Fried Rice Mathematics
- Chilli Con Sausage
- Coronation Chicken Rice Salad

Aquafaba

- Black Forest Mousse

APPENDIX 4 – WHAT TO DO WITH LEFTOVER INGREDIENTS FROM COOK CLEVER RECIPES

Fractions of stock cubes

These can be kept in your store-cupboard, just keep in the foil wrap they came in, or pop into an airtight bag or Tupperware and crumble into cooked dishes for flavour or save for recipes needing ½ cubes.

Fractions of stock pots

Freeze the ½ or ¼ portion of gel-like stock. Just pop onto a tray and allow to open freeze before placing into a labelled ('½ stock cube') resealable freezer bag. Freeze the zest by scattering onto parchment paper on a tray and open freeze, once frozen pop into a labelled ('lime zest') resealable freezer bag. Use from frozen.

Wine

(If there is such a thing) freeze in portions – i.e. tablespoons or teaspoons using ice cube trays. Decant into a labelled ('1 cube = 1 tbsp' for example) resealable freezer bag. Use from frozen in cooked dishes.

Citrus

Freeze fractions in many ways: juice frozen in ice cube trays, slices or segments in a labelled ('½ lime' for example) resealable freezer bag. Use from frozen or defrost if squeezing juice from a segment.

Ghee

Store in the fridge for up to 6 months.

Feta Cheese

Pop into a labelled ('½ block feta cheese') resealable freezer bag and freeze for up to a month. Use in cooked dishes. Defrost in the fridge if in a block or use from frozen if crumbled.

Cream Cheese

Can be stored in its original container and then in a resealable freezer bag for up to 3 months. Defrost in the fridge and use in cooked dishes or whip it to make it creamy again.

Soured Cream

Freeze in portions – i.e. tablespoons or teaspoons – using ice cube trays. Decant into a labelled ('1 cube = 1 tbsp' for example) resealable freezer bag. Use from frozen in cooked dishes. (The texture will be different but it's absolutely fine to use).

Yoghurt

Freeze in portions – i.e. tablespoons or teaspoons – using ice cube trays. Decant into a labelled ('1 cube = 1 tbsp' for example) resealable freezer bag. Use from frozen in cooked dishes. (The texture will be different but it's absolutely fine to use).

Double Cream

Freeze in portions – i.e. tablespoons or teaspoons – using ice cube trays. Decant into a labelled ('1 cube = 1 tbsp' for example) resealable freezer bag for up to 3 months. Use from frozen in cooked dishes. (The texture will be different but it's absolutely fine to use).

Egg whites

Freeze in portions – i.e. 1 egg white – in an ice cube tray. Decant into a labelled ('1 cube = ½ egg white') resealable freezer bags. Defrost overnight in the fridge.

Soft Herbs (parsley/coriander/basil)

Finely snip or chop and scatter onto parchment paper on a tray and open freeze, once frozen pop into a labelled ('chopped parsley' for example) resealable freezer bag. Use in cooked dishes. Use from frozen.

Lemongrass

Either freeze whole in labelled resealable freezer bags and defrost before using in cooked dishes, or remove the woody outer leaves, blitz up in a food processor and freeze in portioned ice cubes (½ stick lemongrass), then once frozen decant into a labelled resealable freezer bag to use straight from frozen in cooked dishes.

Tortilla wraps

Pop into labelled resealable freezer bags and separate each tortilla with parchment paper, or open freeze them on a tray first until frozen solid then pop into the bags. Leave to defrost on the counter for a few minutes whilst you prepare the rest of the dish then warm through in a dry pan or in a hot oven for a few minutes.

Cooked potatoes

Can be frozen whole, pop onto a tray to open freeze then decant into a labelled resealable freezer-proof bag. Can be frozen mashed, just pop straight into a labelled resealable freezer bag and flatten out.

Tinned or jarred cherries in syrup or Kirsch

Freeze any excess syrup in ice cube trays (best frozen in portions of 1 tbsp), then once frozen, decant into a labelled, resealable freezer bag up to 6 months. For the cherries, pop onto a tray lined with parchment paper, open freeze until frozen solid then decant into a labelled, resealable freezer bag. Defrost in the fridge, or if using immediately at room temperature.

Mango/papaya/pineapple

Open freeze on a tray lined with parchment paper then pop into a labelled resealable freezer bag. Use from frozen in smoothies, or defrost in the fridge and use in cooked dishes, like baked goods and desserts.

Tinned olives

Drain away the brine, open freeze on a tray lined with parchment paper and decant into a labelled resealable freezer bag. Use from frozen in cooked dishes or to top pizzas.

Tahini

Store in the fridge for up to a couple of months

Chorizo

Once opened, use within a week, or pop into a labelled resealable freezer bag and use within a month.

Mince

To freeze, pop into a labelled resealable freezer bag. Defrost in the fridge, or if separated into a flat thin piece, crumble straight into cooking dishes.

INDEX

A

B

butter 32
  Garlic Butter 57
  Hasty Hollandaise 193
Buttercup Board, Build Me Up 120–1

C

G

H

I

J

jalapeño peppers
  Cajun Hash Benedict 50
  Jalapeño Hollandaise 193
  Jalapeño Yoghurt Drizzle 158
  Mango Jalapeño Jam 146
  Masala Naan Bread Pizza 90
Jam, Mango Jalapeño 146
Jerk Chicken Strippers 188

K

Kebabs, Mediterranean Chicken 46
kidney beans
  Chilli Con Sausage 48
  Firecracker Quesadillas 42
Kind of Keema Lamb Pau 52

L

Laksa, Lazy 106
lamb
  Crispy Lamb Topping 111
  Kind of Keema Lamb Pau 52
  leftovers 202
  Lemon Olive Oil Lamb & Two Veg 78
Lava Cake, Almost Instant 178
Lazy Laksa 106
leftovers 14, 202–7
  Fried Rice Mathematics 124–5
  Wrapper's Delight 118–19
lemons
  Chorizo Lemon Crumb 153
  Lemon Easecake 179
  Lemon Olive Oil Lamb & Two Veg 78
  Mediterranean Chicken Strippers 188
  One-Tin Spring Roast Chicken 80
  Sa(d)lad Pesto 100

  Watercress Chilli Salsa 159
lemongrass 205
  Firecracker Paste 93
lentils
  Cheatballs 55
  Corn Dumpling Soup 71
lettuce
  Asian Pork Lettuce Wraps 93
  Coronation Chicken Rice Salad 107
limes
  Asian Pork Lettuce Wraps 93
  Bang Bang Sauce 108
  Coconut & Lime Bread Croutons 160
  Crying Tiger(ish) Sauce 149
  Lazy Laksa 106
  Lime Soured Cream 42
  Tamarind Sauce 76

M

Make a Pie Of It 136–7
mangoes 207
  Cheatsy Caribbean (Hot) Pepper Sauce 156
  Mango Jalapeño Jam 146
maple syrup
  Carrot Cake Pancakes 173
Masala Naan Bread Pizza 90
mayonnaise
  Buffalo Roast Cauli 'Potato' Salad 40
  Build Me Up Buttercup Board 120–1
  Caesar-style Dressing 132–3
  Coronation Chicken Rice Salad 107
  Crispy Tofu Asian Loaded Fries 66
  Mayo for Morons 192
  Picnic Loaf 82
  Wrapper's Delight 118–19
measuring in mugs 30
meatballs
  Cheatballs 55
  Spaghetti Meatballs Traybake 64

P

T

V

W

Y

Z

ACKNOWLEDGEMENTS

Oh my, writing this book has been such a delight (except for recipe testing overlapping with some 'gag-tastic' first-trimester spring onion aversion . . .), so a big thank you to my editor extraordinaire (and fellow Gilmore Girl Groupie) Katya Shipster for this joyous opportunity to officially write down the recipes for the food I genuinely make for my family and me, on a day-to-day basis. And to the loveliest team (working with some of you a second time, how lucky am I!) who soaked the simplicity into a stunning design of saturated colour, made meals look magical, styled and photographed the most basic ingredients into beautiful ones, OKed (some of) my not-so-rude puns and made me 'not pregnant' (lols) with a week to go: Sarah Hammond, Sim Greenaway, Andrew Burton, Emily Jonzen and Georgia Rudd, thank you. And of course a big thank you, as always, to my agent (who I pester non-stop), Antony Topping.

To Ben, for such incredible patience and enthusiasm during the testing stage of this book (and himself having to wield his scissors to *Cook Clever* for me on many an occasion when the heartburn and sickness was a bit too much. And, (sorry Ben) if he can do it, anyone can do it. REALLY!, thank you my love. Milesy and Otty, my little taste-testers, your world-class constructive criticism: 'more chocolate'/'this is the best ever', (Jay Rayner, watch out!), had definitive impact on certain of the recipes. To our Littlest Cupcake, boy (or rather, girl) you added an extra dimension of challenge to the writing and testing of this book and I'm tickled pink that I get to share some of the glorious photo spaces of these pages with you.

And to all of you who cook from my recipes, ask for clever tips or give feedback on or share images of the dishes from my books and TV appearances, the most humongous THANK YOU. You give me the inspiration to test, trial and create these recipes! Please stay hungry for more!

HarperCollins*Publishers*
1 London Bridge Street
London SE1 9GF

www.harpercollins.co.uk

HarperCollins*Publishers*
Macken House, 39/40 Mayor Street Upper
Dublin 1, D01 C9W8, Ireland

First published by HarperCollins*Publishers* 2023

10 9 8 7 6 5 4 3 2 1

A catalogue record of this book is available from the British Library

ISBN 978-0-00-855103-2

Food Stylist: Emily Jonzen
Prop Stylist: Lydia McPherson

Printed and bound by GPS

MIX
Paper | Supporting
responsible forestry
FSC™ C007454

This book is produced from independently certified FSC™ paper to
ensure responsible forest management.

For more information visit: www.harpercollins.co.uk/green

WHEN USING KITCHEN APPLIANCES PLEASE ALWAYS FOLLOW
THE MANUFACTURER'S INSTRUCTIONS